Graeme Donald's ea
to agree with his
lesson in semantics led him to Paris, where
women's fashion for two and a half years before
returning to Stockton-on-Tees to run a pub – into
the ground, according to its owners. After a few
years renovating antiques and stripping churches,
his long-abiding passion for word origins demanded
full attention and on this he has concentrated for the
past ten years. Apart from his daily column in *Today*,
his involvement with radio and television includes his
long-running radio series, *Back to Square One*.

The *Today* Book of

Things You Didn't Know You Didn't Know

Graeme Donald

SIMON & SCHUSTER

LONDON·SYDNEY·NEW YORK·TOKYO·SINGAPORE·TORONTO

First published in Great Britain by
Simon & Schuster Ltd in 1992
A Paramount Communications Company

Simon & Schuster Ltd
West Garden Place
Kendal Street
London W2 2AQ

Simon & Schuster of Australia Pty Ltd
Sydney

A CIP catalogue record for this book is
available from the British Library
ISBN 0-671-71175-X

Typeset in Trump Medieval 10/12 by
Hewer Text Composition Services, Edinburgh
Printed and bound in Great Britain by
HarperCollins Manufacturing, Glasgow

For Sue,
with loving thanks for a brighter future

Contents

Misconceptions

To understand why we call the French 'frogs' it is necessary to go back to the days when that which is now called France was part of the Frankish kingdom and was ruled by a man called Clovis.

In AD493 Clovis married a comely wench who rejoiced in the unfortunate name of Clotilda. As soon as she had consolidated her position, Clotilda – who was a staunch Christian on the quiet – came out of the closet and embarked on a remorseless campaign to convert her pagan husband.

Having been systematically beaten about the head with a Bible for seven years, the poor chap realised the hopelessness of his position and gave in. Yes! Jesus could have him for a sunbeam.

No doubt to get a little peace and quiet for a change, he agreed to pop out and smite the Philistine in the shape of the Visigoths, a group of gentlemen who were less than pleased at Clovis's conversion.

En route to the decisive battle, Clovis fancied he had a vision. In it, he saw his heraldic device change from its usual three golden toads on an azure background to three golden lilies. Presuming this to be a hot tip from head office to indicate victory, he ordered such a banner to be made. And under it, he did chastise the Philistine sorely.

Perhaps working on the assumption that anything has got to be better than having a trio of toads cavorting about his banner, Clovis decided to retain the new design, later handing it down as the fleur-de-lis to that which became France.

Much later, when the French court was permanently established at the greatest of all monuments to vulgarity and bad taste, Versailles, the courtiers drew the humorous division of toads and frogs between themselves and the ordinary Parisians. Harking back to the glory of the Frankish kingdom, they considered themselves the toads and always referred to the city dwellers as *Les Grenouilles*, frogs being the smaller of the two species. So it was the French who started calling themselves Frogs. It did not arise as an insult levelled from outside the country due to the Frenchman's repugnant predilection for consuming the nether regions of frogs, as is often asserted.

■ ■ ■

In the early hours of Sunday 2 September 1666, the Great Fire of London broke out at the Pudding Lane premises of Thomas Farynor, the King's baker. The family escaped across the rooftops leaving behind their maid (who was too frightened to move). She became the first of the four to die in the greatest fire in history. That's right, the fire claimed but four lives.

You see, when the plague struck in 1665, London's population was approximately 460,000. Well over two-thirds headed for the hills. Of the rest the plague took some 90,000.

By the time the fire started the population could have been as low as 35–40,000, leaving a ghost town to be consumed by the flames.

The slums that were the plague's stronghold were largely untouched. That exposes as a myth the notion that the fire purged London of the pestilence. It did no such thing. Just for the record, two of the other fatalities were unknowns. The third was Paul Lowell, a watch-maker of Shoe Lane. He believed the dangers to be exaggerated and announced his intention to remain in his home until the roof fell in on him. It did.

Another 'exotic' disease which once haunted these isles was, believe it or not, leprosy. Surprisingly the last indigenous case of leprosy only died in the Shetland Islands at the turn of the nineteenth-century. There are probably some 300 registered cases in England at the moment. But don't worry, leprosy has never been the disease of popular imagination. Nobody 'falls to pieces', and prolonged and very intimate contact with a leper is required before someone catches the infection.

Talking about Scotland and leprosy, did you know that the so-called Robert the Bruce – who died of it – was actually French? His family landed with William the Conqueror, and his real name was Robert de Bruis.

■ ■ ■

There was no baby boom nine months after the 1965 New York blackouts. The birth rate was lower than that of the same period for the previous five years. Perhaps lovers could not find each other in the dark.

Nor was there a rainfall of ex-millionaires committing suicide after the Wall Street Crash – the national and regional suicide rate remained supremely unaffected by the financial disaster.

Still on the subject of suicide, it is a total myth that Sweden has the highest rate; perhaps it was assumed that a race with nothing else to do except watch reruns of Ingmar Bergman films and read porno magazines would surely find death a blessed release.

Actually, it is Hungary that leads the field, with a suicide rate of forty-three per thousand. Forgetting unfair competition like the Vatican, Jordan has claim to the lowest rate: an intriguing 0.4 per cent of a person contrives to pre-empt the Almighty and rush rudely unannounced into his presence. A point to ponder, but that is what the statistics say.

It is often said that suicide is illegal in this country, but this is simply not so. Suicide pacts involving two or more are legislated against, but if you want to pop your clogs you may do so without the worry of picking up a criminal record. Incongruously enough, spring is the most popular time for this somewhat introspective pastime, not the more dismal months of the year.

The birthrate/population density figures also reveal one or two surprises in that China loses all around. The highest birthrate is that of Kenya and, again forgetting the Vatican (at least one would hope so), the lowest rate is to be found in West Germany. Incidentally, the heaviest normal delivery on record is one of twenty-two and a half pounds.

When it comes to the most densely populated country in the world – forgetting city states and principalities like Macao and Monaco – the surprise winner is Bangladesh. Again forgetting 'cheat' entries like the Vatican state, Greenland is the least-densely populated country in the world.

■ ■ ■

Most people think that Samuel Morse invented the telegraph. Perhaps this is because he went around telling everybody that this was the case. In reality he had stolen the idea from Joseph Henry, subsequently denying any knowledge of the man's work. The falsehood was proved to be such in an embarrassingly public court case. However, Morse did invent the code that bears his name, but did you know that when he wanted to plot out the symbols he had to go to his local newspaper for help?

Obviously he wanted to assign the shortest signals to the most commonly used letters, so he asked if he could pop into the print room and count how many of each letter were kept in stock.

The best-known piece of Morse code has got to be SOS but this does not stand for 'Save our Souls' or any of the more colourful, not to mention indecent, alternatives. Strangely enough, it does not even stand for the three letters 'S', 'O', and 'S'. Prior to 1908, when SOS was adopted as the official international distress signal, the code CQD had been employed. CQ on its own meant 'Stand by to receive transmission' and the letter 'D' was added to indicate distress. This did not save the signal from the tortured minds of erstwhile acronymaniacs who promptly started spreading the story that the signal stood for 'Come quick – distress'.

SOS was chosen not because it spelt or represented anything but because it was eminently memorable, recognisable and transmittable at times of stress even by a total novice such as a ship's passenger. Had it spelt nothing at all in Morse, it would still have been chosen. It is transmitted as a pattern, not as a sequence of letters.

The only distress call that does have any etymological story to tell is the verbal 'May Day', which is a corruption of the French *M'aidez* and means 'come and help me'.

The ships least likely to sink were either 'copper-bottomed' or 'A1'. Vessels with copper-clad holds were considered a good insurance risk, which is why today the expression means 'a sure thing'.

Lloyd's Register used to list all commercial shipping and grade each individual vessel according to her condition. Letters designated the state of the hold and numbers the state of the ship's equipment. 'A1' was the highest rating.

■ ■ ■

Solidly fixed in everybody's mind is the image of Atlas the Titan whiling away his time supporting the world on his back, a mistaken image for which we have a sixteenth-century map-maker to thank. Atlas's true fate was to be turned to stone by being forced to look at the Gorgon's head, hence the name of the Atlas mountains, so that he could support the heavens on his back for eternity. This was his punishment for waging war on the Gods of Olympus.

In 1595, Rumold Mercator published an edition of his father's maps, all nicely bound in a special volume. Requiring an impressive cover design, Mercator went for a picture of Atlas on one knee shouldering the troubles of the world. Not only did this fix the myth regarding the giant's fate but it also secured his name forever as the proper term for a book of maps.

It is not easy to think of the word 'Titan' without remembering the RMS *Titanic*'s ill-fated maiden voyage and a little bit of digging reveals a striking coincidence attached to her sinking. Fourteen years before she set sail for history from Southampton, an author called Morgan Robertson published a novel entitled *Futility*. Robertson's book told of a massive liner, also the biggest in its day, named 'Titan'. The fictional ship was also laden with rich passengers for her maiden voyage to America when she strck an iceberg in exactly the same vicinity in the North Atlantic as did the *Titanic* in 1912. In both fiction and fact, the terrible loss of life, significantly amongst the lower-class passengers, was due to a desperate shortage of lifeboats. Those that were available were offered to the first-class passengers and launched half empty. Both ships were short of lifeboats because the builders thought that the compartmentalised construction made them unsinkable.

I have read that several of the passengers' and crew-members' names were also identical but I have been unable to check this in *Futility*.

Finally, it is but as popular myth that the ship's band played 'Nearer My God To Thee' as the ship went down: such a tune would hardly be much of a morale booster under the circumstances. The band actually played ragtime in a vain attempt to jolly things along.

■ ■ ■

The size, prowess and wing span of the Andean condor are nothing as impressive as many suppose. Leaving aside such unfair competition as the ostrich and restricting the field to flying birds alone, the condor, tipping the scales at around the twenty-pound mark and measuring about four feet in length, is heavily out-gunned by various birds. It is difficult to understand why the *Encyclopaedia Britannica*, to name but one reference book, insists on bestowing the accolade of 'largest flying bird' upon the vulturine head of the condor.

The largest wing-span ever recorded was that of a Marabou stork, which boasted a massive span of thirteen feet. But in a species which rarely exceeds nine foot six inches this was admittedly a one-off case. Weighing about the same as a condor, the wandering albatross is generally regarded as the bird with the largest wing span. Even ignoring the odd rogue specimen with a span of twelve feet, the albatross usually averages a comfortable two feet more than the condor's nine-feet wing span.

On the domestic front, we have the swan. An impressive bird by any standards, the mute swan can reach over five feet in length and weigh more than forty pounds. This leaves the condor with only the dubious honour of being the heaviest of the birds of prey.

Birds of prey have given us several expressions. In the days when falconry was popular in Britain, when a hawk achieved its hunting height it was said to be in its 'pride of place'.

When it attacked this was called its 'fell swoop', an expression often uttered incorrectly today as 'foul swoop'. Fell meant cruel, vicious and bloody and felon is an allied term.

Based on a Norman term meaning hedge-dwelling, haggard was used to describe a hawk captured after acquiring its adult plumage. This meant the bird had been hunting for itself far too long for it to be a tameable prospect. Such birds do have a lean and unkempt look about them.

It used to be trendy in London to live in the kind of home which estate agents described as 'intimate and convenient' – in other words, grossly overpriced, cripplingly small and slap bang in the middle of town. Otherwise known as mews cottages, these houses are ultimately named from 'mutate', in that 'mew' described the moulting of hawks, during which they were kept in mews. The price that some people will pay to be, quite literally 'cooped' up!

■　■　■

The Spanish Civil War, like any conflict, spawned its own set of lies, myths and half-truths, and when the Germans bombed Guernica for Franco's forces, all sorts of stories began flying about, such as: the action had been deliberately planned for a busy market day; the town was completely obliterated; Guernica had been picked at random to try out bombing patterns in preparation for the Second World War. All totally false.

Franco had routed substantial numbers of Republican troops, all of whom were in full retreat. Given the direction in which they were heading, no matter which road they took, they were going to bottle-neck at Guernica.

This fact was immediately obvious to their enemies who, quite logically from their point of view, considered the town a legitimate target. Random had nothing to do with it.

As for the image of Guernica packed with happy peasants when the bombs fell, this too is so much nonsense. The average peasant had already worked out for himself exactly what was going to happen and kept well clear of the place, market day or no.

The town was crawling with troops and there was an arms factory there. What did the Republicans expect? An arms factory alone had been sufficient reason for them to bomb flat Durango but a short time before – an action which they did undertake on a busy market day, unannounced, thereby causing massive civilian casualties. This was an incident they never seemed anxious to talk about during all the accusations about Guernica.

It is completely untrue that Guernica was blown off the map. Over half the town was untouched which, considering the small size of the place and the number of people involved, was pretty good going. All said and done, severe damage was inflicted upon the town by a single bombing run that passed from the north-east to the south-west. Since forty per cent of the buildings were flattened in the attack it is a fair assumption that, if the Germans really had wanted to 'remove' the place, then another pass would have done the job. The 'obliteration' part of the myth was greatly reinforced by Picasso's painting of Guernica. Picasso was a staunch Republican who was very careful not to do a painting of what was left of Durango, less than a hour's drive away.

■ ■ ■

In purist terms 'Siamese twins' is something of a misnomer since the pair that gave rise to the designation was actually Chinese, they just happened to be born in Siam.

Chang and Eng became a celebrated double act that, billed as 'The Siamese Twins' toured the world and earned them a small fortune. They eventually settled in North Carolina where they set about making even more money as slave traders, in partnership of course. Yes they did get married – to two sisters in fact. And the answer to your next question is also yes, they had twenty-two children between them. As for the next question which will spring to your lips, I'm sorry one can only speculate but it does bring a whole new meaning to the oft-used phrase about 'two consenting adults'.

The main problem in their private life seems to have been that Chang was inordinately fond of the bottle which made his other half the only teetotal drunk in history.

On the subject of non-white Americans and slavery, things were not as black and white as most imagine. There were many free blacks who operated in private business, usually as slavers themselves. In fact legislation had to be passed to prevent blacks owning white slaves as this was considered quite out of the question and totally unseemly. That's right, white slaves. Until the early nineteenth century whites were enslaved on the plantations as well. Indeed the word 'kidnapping' was first coined back in the seventeenth century to describe the wholesale abduction of children throughout England for shipping to the New World and a life of servitude.

Incidentally, the world 'slave' is simply a variant of 'Slav'; in the Middle Ages the Germans captured so many Slavs and sold them into bondage that Slav came to denote any slave irrespective of nationality.

■ ■ ■

Devil's Island. Now there's a name to chill the hearts of thousands of criminals shipped there to be eaten alive by mosquitoes and giant snakes, or just casually beaten to death by sadistic guards. Strange then, is it not, that the island is only one square mile in area and therefore incapable of holding any such numbers.

The island was named for the hazardous waters around it, not for anything diabolical that happened on it. France did use the place as a penal colony, but strictly for prisoners of a political status. Rarely numbering more than a dozen or so, the inmates had their own cabins, vegetable gardens, fishing tackle and a handy supply of coconut trees. Mail, parcels from home and medical check-ups came regularly by boat and, as for the brutal guards, well there weren't any since the surrounding waters provided the best possible restraint. Despite popular fiction, no common criminals ever enjoyed the conditions there and no escapes from the island are recorded.

Another prison yarn hyped by Hollywood is that of Robert F. Stroud, who was built up to be the Birdman of Alcatraz. Already serving time for murder, Stroud killed a guard in Levenworth prison in 1916 during a dispute over some piffling matter. This was archetypical of the unpredictable and psychopathic twist of his nature. While still at Levenworth, he found four fledgling sparrows in the exercise yard and was allowed to keep them for a short time in his cell. He became interesting in ornithology and, perhaps deciding to kill time instead of people, he read widely on the subject and even wrote a couple of books of moderate merit. All of this took place in Levenworth.

Twenty-two years later in 1942 he was again becoming difficult to handle and was moved to solitary confinement in Alcatraz. Throughout the rest of his life there, which ended on 21 November 1963 with a heart attack, the only birds that Stroud saw were the ones flying past his window – no matter what the Burt Lancaster film shows.

▪ ■ ▪

One of the greatest misconceptions in the field of word origins is that attached to 'posh'.

The story goes that in the days of British India the upper-crust, when travelling to that bastion of Empire, always booked a portside cabin for the outward journey and a starboard one for the return. This supposedly produced an acronym of Port Out Starboard Home. The purpose of so booking with the P&O line was to ensure a shaded cabin for both legs of the trip.

Although this seems to be a beautifully neat explanation, it is nevertheless false. The P&O booking records go back to 1849 and they can not find any evidence of a single posh booking. In addition to this, Mr S. Rabson, the librarian for the P&O company, reveals that the side of the ship in relation to its direction of travel was irrelevant to the price of the cabin, so where are the connotations of wealth and prestige?

Nor would there be any advantage or comfort in booking this way. Your cabin would be in direct sunlight all morning for the majority of the long trip to India, until the Suez Canal opened, of course. After midday, when the heat rose dramatically, it would be all but irrelevant where your cabin was. Besides, who stayed in their cabin all day?

Another misapplied word is 'snob'. The term is rarely applied to the people who conform to the dictionary definition. A snob is not an arrogant type of high social standing who looks down his nose at those he considers beneath him. He is exactly the opposite! A dictionary describes snob as 'a person belonging to the lower classes of society, one having no pretensions to rank or quality' or 'a vulgar or ostentatious person'. To put it bluntly, a snob is a lower-class crawler to the upper classes.

The term developed in the early days at Oxford and Cambridge Universities, where new students not only had to register their names, but also their ranks. Those of noble birth were required to log their title and those not so elevated of station were obliged to put *sine nobilitae*, the Latin for 'without nobility'. This was later abbreviated to 's. nob', and snob was coined by the titled students to describe the untitled students who kept trying to mix with the nobs and ingratiate themselves.

■ ■ ■

The last time men were sentenced by a British court to be drawn, hanged and quartered (no, not hanged, drawn and quartered as is always incorrectly stated) was just over one hundred years ago. In 1867 three Fenians received the repugnant penalty but were subsequently let off with a simple hanging.

A typical reading of the sentence was as follows: 'You are to be *drawn* on hurdles to the place of execution where you are to be *hanged* but not till you are dead; for, while still living, your body is to be taken down, your bowels torn out and burnt before your face; [this is probably where the confusion arose, from the notion of intestines being 'drawn' out] your head is then to be cut off, and your body divided into four *quarters*.'

A goodly number of miscreants once hung around at Tyburn gibbet or went for a quick walk around the block there. Originally the killing ground stood to the west of the old city of London, on a site corresponding to modern Marble Arch. In old thieves' cant 'gone west' described a terminally absent business associate who had gone for a spin in the municipal tumbril.

I must tell you about the bizarre murder trial of Alfred Packer who can claim not only the unsavoury distinction of being the first man in the United States to face charges of murder and cannibalism, but also that of the first man in history to eradicate an entire political group in a constituency by such an unusual method.

In the winter of 1873, Packer acted as guide to a group of men intent on prospecting the San Juan Mountains in Colorado. The blizzard came hard and early, leaving the party trapped in a shack with limited supplies. Packer realised very quickly that the only real food that he was going to see before the spring was stamping around the cabin complaining about his lousy organisation.

Standing trial ten years after the event, Packer was extremely lucky that the Colorado constitution did not provide for the death penalty. The judge, Edwin Cade, as the spearhead of the Democratic thrust against the predominantly Republican Colorado, felt that he had a personal grievance against the defender. Sentencing Packer for forty years Cade said: 'Packer, you are a low-down, depraved son of a bitch. There were only four Democrats in the whole of Hinsdale County – and you ate all of them.'

■ ■ ■

If there's one thing we all know about the Japanese it is that they all unsportingly sneaked out of the jungle behind Singapore, and that they were falling over each other to volunteer for the Kamikaze. Sorry, wrong again.

Virtually all artillery at Singapore could pan through 360° and some guns shelled the Japanese for three solid days. Singapore fell because the Japanese forces were superior and the British organisation was about as much use as a chocolate teapot. It is myth that Singapore only fell because we believed the jungle was impenetrable and therefore locked all batteries seaward. People preferred to believe the loss a cruel irony so that they wouldn't have to recognise it as the crippling defeat that it really was.

Their effectiveness grossly exaggerated by cinema and time, the Kamikaze were conscripted to a man; not even the Japanese were in that much of a hurry for an honourable end. The pilots were young, expendable, almost totally untrained, and the planes they flew were fit only for the scrap heap. *En route* to target zones they had to keep to the speed of the slowest which made them vulnerable to fighter attack. The Kamikaze flew largely unarmed civil craft. Those that made it to a target area were easy meat for a trained ship's gunners since they were slow-flying and totally unskilled in evasive tactics.

Sometimes they didn't find anyone to crash into; there's one lucky man living in Kyoto who flew eleven Kamikaze missions in the Pacific and that's got to be a record. In all, over 2,300 Kamikaze missions were launched, some comprising more than 300 planes and, although they damaged quite a few ships, they only sank thirty-four. They took their name from an ancient incident when a typhoon destroyed a massive Mongol fleet sent against Japan. 'Kamikaze' means 'Divine Wind'. History doesn't record what the Mongols called the storm which is probably just as well.

■ ■ ■

Quicklime will not accelerate the decomposition of a human body. If anything it will act as a preservative. Lime is hygroscopic which means that it pulls in moisture from its surroundings and generates heat. Lime placed around a body will draw its moisture from that source, producing a kind of mummification – which is the sort of evidence that most murderers dislike.

There is a further disadvantage to packing corpses in lime. All the little creatures that would otherwise speed the reduction of a dead body stay well clear, being reluctant to chomp through the lime.

Nor, while on quick matters, does quicksand suck people under to a horrible death. Quicksand is actually a water-saturated area of sand – water that has not come down as rain but has risen up from beneath the sand under low pressure. In this 'suspended' state, the grains of sand are frictionless and will support no weight. Quicksand is, if you like, extremely sandy water. Under no circumstances will quicksand suck people under. It is the victims who generate the suction. Not unnaturally, anyone caught in it immediately begins to struggle. But as it is a wet environment devoid of any air, any attempt to extricate one foot will only cause downwards pressure on the other one. It is a nastier version of getting your wellingtons stuck in the mud.

Believe it or not, it is actually impossible to sink below the surface of a quicksand bog. As it is saturated sand it is three times more buoyant than water. This means that, unless you're carrying a heavy load, you'll float at a line near your armpits. The only way your head will go under is if you raise your arms above your head. Calm is your best weapon against quicksand.

As soon as you realise your predicament, divest any excess weight such as rucksacks. You'll have plenty of time to do this, so don't panic. Next, irrational as it might sound, lie down flat on your back and with the body weight so distributed, roll back to terra firma.

■ ■ ■

Despite the light and woolly consistency of gooseberry fool, stupidity does not enter the question. The dish is prepared by mashing up the fruit with cream and forcing the resultant mush through a sieve. 'Fool' is a corruption of *foule*, that being the French for pressing or crushing.

Nor does the expression 'playing gooseberry' hold any meaning of a third and unwanted party souring a set-up, although that is its usual application today. In the summertime of yester-year, when the countryside of Old England was teaming with courting couples, some might be lucky enough to be accompanied by a chaperon who would make a point of wandering off for a short time to collect gooseberries and allow the lovers a little time on their own. At other times of year, romantically inclined chaperons would disappear for a short time to 'play' at gathering non-existent gooseberries. So the expression actually describes someone who sweetens the situation for a couple, not the reverse.

Incidentally there is no connection between the name of the berry and geese. The name comes via the French *groseille* and is ultimately derived from the German *kraus*, which means crisp.

On the subject of our forefathers' sex lives, *droit*

de seigneur is a total myth. The enforcement of the so-called right of the first night has been included in many a film. But, alas for the would-be serf-riding barons and war-lords, it never existed. All references in ancient documents indicate that no one took it seriously even then, although sometimes a tongue-in-cheek ritual was enacted during which the groom paid a nominal fee to his lord to forego a 'right' that could not be enforced in any case.

Although many museums display chastity belts, the idea of wanton wives being locked up in metal underwear while their husbands sliced up Saracens is another fallacy. The belts were never intended to be anything other than a joke, or maybe a token to be hung on the wall while the husband was off at war or whatever. Museums display them only as curios for, if one thinks of the natural body functions, a chastity belt is anything but a practical proposition. The best analogy that springs to mind is of some future civilisation displaying in all seriousness the willy-warmers that are so popular as jokes today.

■　■　■

One of the stock scenes of romantic tragedy and soap operas is that of the pregnant heroine taking a tumble on the stairs (preferably long, sweeping marble ones) and starting to miscarry within seconds of landing in an elegantly languid position at the bottom without a hair out of place or a blemish to the exquisitely made-up face. Utter rubbish.

Babies are probably never as safe as when they are in the womb and are not going to be bothered in the slightest by such an incident, unless they are asleep and happen to be rudely awoken. A really heavy and protracted fall could cause some separation between the wall of the uterus and the placenta which would result in bleeding, but not even this unlikely event is going to cause the immediate onset of labour which, in films, always culminates with a stillborn child.

To stand any chance of bringing on labour by such a fall, the mother would have to fall from quite a height and the result may be that she would burst her waters. Since she would have to be well advanced to effect this, there is no reason why the baby should not be born alive and kicking. In effect, the only person likely to suffer injury on the stairs is the mother herself.

Another puzzling thing about silver-screen pregnancies is that as soon as delivery is imminent, everybody starts to charge around boiling horrendous quantities of water. What on earth for? There is nothing to sterilise, nobody is going to scrub-up in boiling water and, hopefully, no one is going to clean-up the arrival with scalding water. Perhaps it is for a celebratory tea party.

And how many women have been forced to glut themselves because of the 'eating for two' myth? In total a pregnant woman needs an additional 80,000 calories over the gestation period. But recent research has shown that during pregnancy the female is more proficient at extracting nutrients and vitamins leaving an increase in food intake unnecessary – providing that the woman eats a sensible and balanced diet in the first place. Nor should a pregnant woman eating properly need to take vitamins. No one should need to, although in the case of a mother-to-be it is perhaps

sensible to take a low strength multi-vitamin to make
sure the system wants for nothing.

■ ■ ■

No one has ever seen a bride walk down the aisle on
her wedding day, not unless she has got hopelessly lost.
The central passage she walks down is called the nave,
the aisles are the other two passages flanking it.

Our ancestors believed the deities of confusion
and mis-rule would attempt to disrupt a wedding
on principle and that their main target would be the
bride. To confuse the would-be confusors, the bride
was always surrounded by a group of girls her own
age, identically dressed and veiled. These girls survive
as the modern bridesmaid.

Brides are carried over the threshold because, although
Janus was the God of the doorway (hence 'janitor' and
'January'), Vesta, of virgin fame, was the goddess of
the hearth and threshold. It was considered unseemly
for a maiden about to lose such claim to tread on the
province of Vesta.

'Honeymoon' derives from the Scandinavian and
Germanic custom in which newly-weds drank a mixture of herbs, honey and wine for one moon after the
nuptials, this being considered necessary to sustain
the protracted bouts of horizontal jogging that are
prone to take place at such time.

Not everyone found this brew to be beneficial.
Paying scant regard to the dangers of marrying Ildico,
a girl less than half his age, Attila the Hun tarried
long at his wedding feast quaffing such terrifying
quantities of the stuff that his followers thought

their leader would be a widower by morning. Just the reverse happened. The greatest liberal ever produced by Germany staggered to his 'hunimoon' bed only to gallop off into history forever. The scourge of Rome died of a heart attack, well and truly laid low by a slip of a girl.

Did you know that the Hollywood-engendered image of Attila as the archetypical brick-built barbarian could not be further from the truth? In reality he looked like the little, red-bearded character out of the Bugs Bunny cartoons. He was a barrel-chested dwarf with a disproportionately large head, a bright-red, turned-up snout of a nose and deep-set bulging eyes. Not a pretty sight.

■   ▪   ■

The current patterns of Fair Isle knitting are another influence exerted on our culture by the Moors.

In the sixteenth century Phillip II of Spain dispatched his ill-fated Armada against England. Fortunately for us he placed it under the command of a court favourite with all the tactical and command capabilities of a telephone box, the Duc Medina Sidonia.

After Drake and his Plymouth Hoe Crown Green Bowling Association had put paid to the Duc's aspirations, a flotilla of British ships pursued the survivors relentlessly northward. Those that did not sink were wrecked on the treacherous rocks off the Orkney and Shetland Isles. The hospitable islanders slaughtered any that made it to their shores and stripped their ships of anything of value or use. On Fair Isle, where the history and tradition of the island were 'written' into the knitting patterns due to all-pervasive illiteracy, this had the effect of exposing the islanders to the rich and intricate Moorish designs on the clothing and possessions of their victims. There is even one design called the Armada Cross.

Whilst talking about the Scottish it is unfair to hold them responsible for the bagpipes for these are most likely of Persian origin, and brought here by the Celts in the Bronze Age. They reached their height of development in the Scottish regiments as a weapon of war and not a musical instrument. Used to strike fear into the heart of the Sassenach foes before battle was joined, it was a precursor of today's modern stun grenades.

The haggis too is held by some to have invaded our shores. This time the Romans are hailed as the culprits. They devised it as ideal rations for an army on the move. The Scots maintain this to be a.vile slander and point out that they had little contact with the Romans who, quite wisely, stayed south of the border and picked on the English who were easier meat.

■ ■ ■

If you think that the death sentence has been abolished in this country, you are wrong. It may have been abolished for murder but it is still very much available for acts of treason and piracy with violence (including airline hijacks). Until 1971, arson in a naval dockyard also carried the death penalty. The only people who cannot be hanged under any circumstances are pregnant women.

It is also widely believed that people surviving the gibbet were automatically entitled to a reprieve. Not so. Most were dragged back for an action-replay. It is fair to say that reprieves were granted on rare occasions for humanitarian reasons but it has never been a legal right. As recently as 1935, an American murderer named Bullen was found running around the morgue after spending some time with Old Sparky. He was persuaded to perform a second time . . .

The great myth attached to the electric chair and reinforced by countless gangster movies, is that the prison lights dim and flicker every time that they are 'frying tonight'. Can you think of anything more ludicrous to permit in the psychological powder-keg of death row? In fact the chair works by creating a massive short-circuit so it would be impossible for it to be linked to the regular supply without it blowing every fuse in the prison.

Another popular if gruesome belief is that witches were burnt at the stake in Merrie England. Not one was. What the poor creatures went through before the blessed release of the noose is best left unsaid but no witches were burnt on either side of the Atlantic. That includes the Salem farce where nineteen were hanged and one pressed to death with rocks.

However, certain crimes were punishable by boiling or burning. Any woman plotting, attempting or committing the murder of her husband could be burnt at the stake since her crime counted as petty treason. Lesser transgressions only warranted the miscreant being obliged to stand in boiling water, the depth of which was directly proportional to the crime. Hence the expression 'From hell and high water may the good Lord deliver us.'

■ ■ ■

Everyone knows that chameleons can change colours to suit their environment. Once again the elusive 'everyone' is wrong. Chameleons can go through some very limited colour changes but the animal never has any choice in the matter since changes are instigated by factors like temperature, light and emotional states such as fear. If you crept up behind a chameleon and shouted 'boo' it would turn exactly the same colour be it on a red carpet or a snooker table.

Another thing that everybody thought they knew about animals is that possums or more exactly opossums play dead when attacked. Perhaps someone ought to tell the possum. Being somewhat larger than a cat and possessed of a full set of rather nasty nashers, far from lying doggo possums will make skilful use of said incisors. It is true that if pursued, tormented and cornered in fear of its life a possum, just like many other animals, will collapse. In humans it's called fainting with fear. As a defence mechanism it leaves a great deal of room for improvement. Faced with a collapsed possum any predator simply thanks its quarry for being so jolly sporting and sits down to lunch.

While we are in the animal kingdom let us forget all those myths about elephants. They may well remember things for a long time but that is just because they happen to live for a long time. Their memory is no better than any other creature with a proportionately sized brain. Nor is the elephant the intellectual giant of popular imagination. True, it can be taught basic commands and certain tricks but nothing as complicated as the daily routine of a good sheep-dog.

As for the elephant's twenty-month pregnancy this is not the world record as many believe. The Alpine black salamander is left holding the baby for three years and two months. Talking about size and reproduction, big is not necessarily best. Under controlled conditions a male jird, a kind of gerbil, mated 224 times in under two hours. This would not only suggest a deplorable lack of self-control in the species but it also explains why there are so many little jirds in Africa.

■ ■ ■

Shipping and the Sea

There is an amusing but false theory which maintains that the naval dog-watch is so named because it is shorter than all the other regular watches and can therefore be regarded as 'curtailed'. Nice story, but that's all it is – a story.

A standard watch at sea lasts for four hours but the two dog-watches which span from 4 till 6pm and from 6 till 8pm, are only two hours long and are either named from a corruption of 'docked' or 'dodge'.

The latter does seem to make the most sense in that it marries nicely with the reason for the shortened watches being instituted. They give an uneven number of watch shifts to a twenty-four-hour period – seven instead of six – so that the watchkeepers, no matter whether they are covering a batch of two or three watches, never cover the same watch day after day. Thus they 'dodged' round the rota.

The origin of 'dead reckoning' is similarly debated but the likely origin is a corruption of 'deduced reckoning'. This is a co-ordinate arrived at by the ship's navigators taking into account speed, direction of travel, current and drift factor to forecast where the ship will be at some point in the future, or where it was at some point in time in the past. Although such calculations do place the ship metaphorically 'dead' in the water, this seems to have had no bearing (no pun intended) on the expression.

■ ■ ■

Modern anchor design largely obviates the need for repeated strikes at the seabed to secure a hold, but in the old days when anchors were little more than weighted hooks, luck played a large part in securing good anchorage. The splayed hooks on an anchor are known as flukes, hence 'a lucky fluke' as describing a chance shot that scores.

If on the other hand the anchor's own cable becomes entangled on the hook *en route* to the seabed this is called a foul-up, and we all know how that feels! For reasons best known to the powers that be, the fouled anchor – a seaman's nightmare – has long been the symbol of the office of the Lord High Admiral.

Landlubbers have also acquired another piece of 'foul' language from sailors – the expression that talks of 'falling foul' of someone or something. In a narrow shipping lane it is common for a faster vessel to find itself impeded by a slower one and with no room to 'overtake'. Under these circumstances the hindmost vessel is said to have fallen foul of the other.

On the subject of objects following one another, this is the only situation in which the expression 'in tandem' is properly applied. Despite its widespread use to denote things placed abreast or tasks undertaken in parallel, this is misuse. The expression was coined as a joke in eighteenth-century university circles and is a play on the Latin *tandem* which does mean 'at length', but only in the context of time. It was first applied to horses placed one behind the other in harness and when the nineteenth-century bicycle arrived the term simply transferred.

The largest tandem-style bike ever built was the twenty-eight-seater constructed for the teacher training college at Zug in Switzerland. The aspiring mentors sat two abreast and went for instructional rides in the country.

■ ■ ■

Back in the days of sail, salted pork was pretty much a standard ration which was stored on board in barrels sealed with a lining of fat. In the event of provisions running low, hungry matelots were reduced to rooting back through previously discarded barrels in a hunt for scraps stuck in the bottom layer of fat and so ignored in better times. This rather undignified behaviour produced 'scraping the bottom of the barrel'.

Under normal conditions this fat, and that produced from the boiling down of any fresh meat brought on board at port of call, was stored up by the ship's cook. Believe it or not, this mushy fat, known as slush, was highly prized by the cook and the purser, to whom it was a perk of the job. From it they made candles which were sold at the next port of call, the two men proceeding to get drunk on the benefits of the 'slush fund'.

Talk of salting money away is also reference to old meat preservation methods in which salt played a great part.

Although today only pepper particles are called

corns, in the old days salt granules were also so known, hence 'corned beef' – that which has been laid up in salt.

The corn on your foot although similar in shape takes its name instead from the Latin *cornu*, animal's horn, and alludes to the hard and horny texture of the growth. Similarly, the cornea, in comparison to the rest of the eye, was considered to be hard of texture.

■ ■ ■

It is only in comparatively recent times that much of the world's waters have been charted and before this the negotiating of unknown shallows and channels was fraught with danger. It was very much a case of dead slow ahead with a chap at the prow furiously taking depth readings which he called out to the skipper. As the vessel's draught began to match the water's depth she scraped over sand-bars and coral projections and only the bravest pressed on, hence 'touch and go' now describing a dodgy situation loaded with risk.

Sometimes the risk paid off and sometimes the ship came unstuck, or, to be more accurate, well and truly stuck on a reef or sand-bar. She was then said to be 'hard and fast', her inflexibility of position causing this designation to transfer to rules that can not be bent under any circumstances. Sometimes the rising tide would come to the aid of a vessel so impeded and lift her high enough to clear the obstacle. Still today we ask for a little help – usually financial – to 'tide us over' some problem or other.

As for our chum at the prow taking the readings,

his activity produced talk of 'swinging the lead' as aimed at malingerers. As the ship nuzzled its perilous way through the waters the crew were required to leap about like the flies possessed of the proverbial azure anatomy as they made various alterations to the set of the sails and what have you to the barked commands from the bridge. Although it is in fact quite strenuous work, by comparison, their comrade with the lead-line had a pretty easy time of it.

The French for lead is *plomb*, hence the metaphorical 'plumbing the depths', not to mention 'plumb line' and 'plumber', such trade developing in the days when all pipes were made of lead.

■ ■ ■

Those with nothing to do are frequently referred to as being 'at a loose end' and, not surprisingly since you're now reading this section, this expression too has a naval origin. Sailors with no specific duties or even those off duty would sit about on deck mending old ropes which had frayed at the ends. Needless to say, the image of a rope hanging over the side of the ship swaying nonchalantly in the breeze will not have hindered the expression's passage into general phraseology. Also from a sailor's day-off comes 'make-do and mend', the popular yet erroneous rendition of the original 'make, do and mend'. Increasingly the former is heard in the context of having to get the job done with whatever inadequate material is to hand, yet to the sailor this was the free day when he got round to making odd bits of equipment he needed, doing all those little tasks that had built up over the week, and mending clothing and personal effects.

The modern 'lose your rag' seems to be a humorous play on the old seafaring expression 'he's lost his cloth', this being said of any ship's captain in a stonking bad mood and the cloth in question being that covering the table in the officers' mess. Should relationships between a captain and his officers break down to such an extent that he wishes to be rid of them, the rules of the Customs of the Sea demand that he indicate such by the removal of the table-cloth. So, without getting into further argument likely to exacerbate the situation the captain may indicate that he has had enough. This gives the officers three days to discuss whether they will apologize and step down or stick to their guns and request to be put ashore.

■ ■ ■

As still used of the barge-like receptacles we sometimes place outside our houses for the benefit of our neighbours, the word 'skip' was an earlier form of 'ship', hence a ship's captain being affectionately referred to as the skipper.

During the sixteenth century, English adopted the French term *esquiper*, which meant to provision a ship prior to departure. The word survives today as 'equipment', such shift in application being occasioned by the nature of much of the gear taken on board, food being a rather small proportion.

Fresh water was of course a prime requirement, this being stored below in huge vats. For daily use by the crew there was on deck a normal-sized barrel with a hole cut about three-quarters of the way up its side. This prevented overfilling at the main vat and wasteful spillage during the transfer back to the deck. This impromptu surgery bestowed upon the barrel the name of 'scuttlebutt', a term which soon transferred to the gossip exchanged by sailors standing about it having a drink.

The term 'scuttle' properly denotes a hole cut out and, on a sailing ship, denoted only a cabin window or the hatchways allowing passage throughout the below-deck areas. The landlubbers' 'porthole' denotes not a cabin window but the hole in the side through which the cannon were aimed.

As a verb meaning to move rapidly and erratically the term could well derive from the movements of sailors lurching through the cramped deck-scuttles or from the darting of a rabbit as seen from behind with its tail, or scut, bobbing up and down. But, since the rabbit's tail is so named from its being cut down, all the terms are somehow related at the end of the day.

■ ■ ■

No sailing ship can function without the help of the block and tackle which does everything from raising and lowering the sails to the loading and unloading. When all the hoisting capacity on the rope has been exploited the block comes hard up against the chock, thus creating the expression 'chock-a-block' describing things crammed in tight.

The only way to free the device was to pass the hauling lines back through the sheaves, these being the pulley holes in the blocks, and then back-haul to separate the components. The very mechanics of the process are admirably reflected in the designation 'over-hauling' which soon spread to the taking apart of any piece of equipment to effect repair.

We also talk of the excessively ambitious 'over-reaching' themselves but it is unclear whether this is derived from things maritime or from the world of horse racing. A sailing ship is described as 'reaching' when she is setting a smart pace with all sails full, but there does come a point when too much sail creates the seafaring equivalent of over-egging the pudding and the ship is slowed by being almost pushed downward into the water. Another expression used of those with more mouth than trousers talks of them 'carrying too much canvas' which amounts to the same thing.

The claim of origination from the fraternity of the turf is equally convincing. When a racing horse lengthens its stride to increase speed it is not unknown for inexperienced and over-enthusiastic animals to 'reach' so much that their hind hooves begin to clatter against the fore ones resulting in the mount falling over its own feet.

■ ■ ■

When the weather cuts up rough at sea, those who find themselves adopting a Robespierreian complexion quit the decks and head below to find a position more central to the ship's mass where the motion is at a minimum. Away from the wind and rain they are then said to be 'under the weather', an expression that came ashore to describe anyone feeling queasy.

Like farmers, sailors are never quite happy with the weather. When a vessel fell becalmed the crew would gather on deck and whistle, believing that such collective activity would raise the wind again. Needless to say the success of such tactics was minimal causing 'you can whistle for it' to enter the realms of phraseology to denote a vain hope.

As for 'clean as a whistle', there have in recent times been attempts to hail this as a corruption of 'clean as a whittle', this being a cut made in a piece of wood during casual carving. Modern production methods and materials have made the manufacture of perfect whistles cheap and easy, but the expression was coined in America when all whistles were hand-made from wood. If the inside surfaces were not free from imperfections and little burrs then the note would not be well defined. So the inside had to be 'clean' in the old sense of the word as meaning unhindered, this same application arising in 'to show a clean pair of heels' or 'to get clean away'.

■ ■ ■

The attitude of sailors towards women is ambivalent to say the least. On the one hand there is a veritable host of maritime superstition perceiving women as unlucky, yet they were of old frequently held captive on board as a defence against storms.

The less than sophisticated seamen of old believed that the sea grew angry at the sight of a woman yet was pacified at the sight of a naked one. This ridiculous belief resulted in countless women being kidnapped and held below decks, only seeing the light of day when they were stripped and lashed to the prow during storms. What happened to these unfortunates below decks is best left unsaid. However, this does explain why so many figureheads are representations of naked or semi-naked women.

Another groundless belief held by sailors . . . come to think of it, they held dear so many idiotic beliefs proved untrue by daily events with such monotonous regularity that one wonders about their sanity . . . was that an angry sea could be mollified by its being anointed with holy oil. Consequently most ships carried a suitable container whose contents could be poured over the side to appease the gods of the deep.

Quite why these superstitious dorks should think pagan deities would be chuffed to little mint balls by having poured on their heads a slimy substance blessed by the organisation that was capriciously incinerating their ever-diminishing fan clubs is another matter, but there you have it. The only positive result of this quaint little ritual was the installation in the language of 'to pour oil on troubled waters'.

■ ■ ■

A modern ships' log is now used to record all pertinent details of the journey, but the book takes its name from earlier days when its only purpose was to record details of routine speed checks taken through the day.

The ship's speedo of yester-year consisted of a chap standing at the prow armed with a log and a length of line in which knots had been tied at intervals of forty-seven feet three inches. On the command, he lobbed the log over the side and counted how many knots were dragged out on the line during a span of twenty-eight seconds, as measured by a sand-glass at his side. Not only does this account for the book's name but also for the habit of expressing a ship's speed in knots.

It is probably fair to say that most imagine the nautical mile to be a fixed measure like its terra firma counterpart. Not so. It is defined as being that distance of the ocean's surface subtended by one minute of latitude at the earth's centre. Because the earth is an oblate spheroid bulging at the equator and flattening off at the poles, a nautical mile is shorter at the former location and longer at the latter.

■　■　■

A rather natty little practice at sea contributed to the language the expression that talks of those conned being 'stitched up'.

When preparing a body for burial at sea it was the practice for the corpse to be first sewn into a canvas shroud to make it easier to consign it to the deep. To ensue that their fellow sea-dog was really dead and not deeply unconscious the last stitch was passed through the divide of the nostrils on the grounds that if anything was going to make you sit up and take notice then that was it. I'm sure they were right. Anyway, the departed sewn into his new mummy-style outfit was deemed properly 'stitched up'.

Navy regulations covering the disposal of bodies at sea decree that such must take place in a minimum of six fathoms, hence death being known as 'the deep six', there being no connection to land graves which, contrary to popular belief, have never been required by law to be dug to a depth of six feet.

As for marriage at sea by the ship's captain on a moonlit quarter deck, this too is shrouded in misconception. Despite it having furnished the dewy-eyed romantic content in countless films and novels, it simply can not happen and never has. And for very sound legal reasons.

Having said that it must also be stated that so deeply entrenched is this myth that certain captain's guides and 'bibles' of ships' business make a point of reminding skippers that they do not have the power to perform any marriage of any kind. Moreover, they should refuse to allow any such ceremony to take place aboard their vessel even if presided over by a fully ordained minister of the cloth, should there happen to be one on hand willing to officiate.

Imagine, if you can, the complications arising from, shall we say, a French woman wishing to marry an Italian in a ceremony run by a Greek priest on board a British ship that lay in German national waters at the time – or, even worse, International Waters! Where, if anywhere, would the marriage be considered valid?

■ ■ ■

Lazy people are frequently called 'wasters', this spelling being born of the misconception that the term is based on their wasting time – but the original and proper form is 'waister'.

On a sailing ship the waist was that area lying in

the middle of the upper deck between the quarter-deck and the forecastle. Here 'worked' the sick, the injured and the malingerers who did little more than deck-swabbing and rope mending. Needless to say, 'waister' was coined by the full-duty sailors.

Another term much misunderstood by land-dwellers is 'AB' which is widely thought to stand for 'Able-Bodied'. This misconception is little hindered by the usual presentation of 'A.B.', but the letters are in fact only the first two of 'able' which indicates the holder's 'ability' to carry out all fundamental duties of a seaman.

On the subject of people being able-bodied in the accepted sense of the phrase, it is often asked why so many pirates are depicted with eyes, legs and various other bits and pieces missing. In such times there were no personal injury plans or policies and disabled sailors who knew nothing but the sea had only piracy to turn to when invalided out by the regular service. Common amongst gunners was blinding by powder-flash, hence the eye-patch and the massive 'splinters' that sheared from the inside of a hull hit with cannonshot were highly likely to leave a man with a peg-leg.

As for the obligatory golden ring in the ear few pirates went in for such theatricals — if for no other reasons than it gave an adversary a very painful handhold and it was too easy for a thief to rip it off with equally painful consequences. Far safer and practical was the fashion of braiding it into their hair and its sole purpose was to ensure that the ever-superstitious sailor was never to be without the wherewithal to pay for his own Christian burial.

■ ■ ■

It seems that as soon as someone acquires fame then the myth-makers immediately set to work inventing quotes and apposite apocrypha to gild the lily – actually, the proper quotation from Shakespeare's *The Life and Death of King John*, Act IV, scene 2, line 11, is: 'To gild refined gold, to paint the lily,' – but that, as they say, is another story. England's most famous seafaring chappie was without doubt Horatio Nelson, and there has been an awful lot of guff and hot air blown about him.

Most famous is of course the yarn concerning the telescope to the blind eye and the announcement 'I see no signal', yet to be fair, this did in fact happen although not in the way imagined. It was actually a joke played by Nelson on those nearby.

The scene was the Battle of Copenhagen (1801) and Nelson was under the command of Admiral Sir Hyde Parker, who, prior to the engagement, had informed Nelson that he would be the man in the thick of it and thus best placed to judge whether to continue the fight or cut and run. Parker went on to say that should things begin to look a bit sticky he would raise a signal to disengage but that Nelson could regard any such signal as permissive. Thus it was an 'out' for Nelson should he feel he needed it, but he was free to continue the fight should he so desire and Parker would assume responsibility either way. The fiasco with the telescope to the blind eye was a joke at the expense of the nearby Marine Colonel Stewart who was unaware of the verbal overrider to

the signal. Let's face it – the Navy never could resist
a dig at the Army.

■ ■ ■

Many generations of wide-eyed British schoolboys
have sat and listened to stern lectures on responsibility and duty being pointed up by the stirring
tale of Nelson and his flag signal informing the fleet
just before the kick-off of the Battle of Trafalgar that
'England expects that every man will do his duty.' As
always, things were not quite as imagined on the big
day itself!

First of all it must be stated that this most famous
of all flag signals in British history may have been
used to stir the blood of later generations but the
people to whom it was directed took it as a deeply
wounding insult implying that they needed reminding
as to where lay their duty. Vice Admiral Collingwood
is noted as saying something along the lines of 'I wish
Nelson would stop all this bloody signalling and get
on with the job; we are all, I am sure, fully aware
what is expected of us today.'

Even more entertaining is the fact that, like so
many other great moments in history, the signal
itself was born in something akin to farce. First
of all Nelson called for Lt Pasco, the signals officer,
and demanded the raising of 'Nelson confides' etc.
which was greeted with mild clearing of throats and
the tentative suggestion from attendant officers that
perhaps 'England confides' etc. might sound better.
Nelson agreed and ordered the amended signal to be
made, but there were more problems ahead. Pasco

returned to announce he had no flag for 'confides' which would therefore need spelling out, but he did have a flag for 'expects' and could he please make a substitution. Nelson, now heartily sick of the whole business and no doubt wishing he had never been beset by such high-falutin sentiments, snapped something along the lines of 'Whatever you want – just send the damn signal.'

■ ■ ■

There has been much debate regarding Nelson's last words. That the last discernible sentence began with the words 'I thank God I have done my duty . . .' is likely beyond debate, but were the second and final sentence the much-mimicked 'Kiss me, Hardy' or 'Kismet, Hardy'?

Despite the notion that long periods at sea are apt to warp a fellow, the former does seem the less likely of the two. Although as a word 'Kismet' was extremely rare in English prior to 1850 (Trafalgar was fought in 1805), Nelson had spent a fair amount of time around Egypt and Malta where the Arabic tongue – whence 'kismet' comes – is widely spoken. The term properly means not just fate but the end, or the fulfilment, of one's allotted span or portion so it would have been a highly apposite word for Nelson to use leaving those around him less familiar with the term to misinterpret due to the all-pervasive sound of battle.

It is also regrettably untrue that the motto of the Comte de Villeneuve, commander of the French squadron at Trafalgar, translates as 'To The Water –

This Is The Hour'. Would that it were, for in the original French this would appear as *A L'Eau – C'Est L'Heure!*.

At the risk of appearing to pick on folklore and popular tradition it is also necessary to point out that Horatio Nelson never lost an eye nor did he ever once wear an eye-patch.

His right eye was wounded during the occupation of Corsica in 1794 and, although it healed, the sight faded rapidly. Nevertheless, the only visual aid he ever employed was a shade clipped to his hat.

■ ■ ■

Many the Roman epic depicted chained slaves rowing their little hearts out in Roman galleys to the sombre yet ominously monotone beat generated by a stern-faced Nubian thumping away on a massive drum. But then Hollywood has never been a town to permit the truth to get in the way of a few bucks.

To begin with, mast and sail were used while under passage since even a crew in peak condition would have been hard pressed to row a galley much more than ten miles without collapsing, and these men needed to conserve their strength for the considerable effort required to manoeuvre the vessel and crank her up to the maximum speed of about ten knots to ram the enemy. The emaciated souls of celluloid fame wouldn't have managed ten oar strokes.

The rowing crew, sometimes as many as two hundred in the case of a trireme, formed the greater part of a boarding party so a Roman galley commander was hardly likely to relish the prospect of unchaining in battle two hundred resentful slaves and felons who had more to gain from joining the enemy than fighting for Rome and the continuance of their own servitude.

As for the huge, leopard-skin clad Nubian time-keeper, he too is of modern imagination. Sharp sound-ing drums that could throw their note any distance at all did not emerge until the fourteenth century, and the dull, flat-sounding drum the Romans used would not have been heard from one end of the rowing deck to the other let alone throughout the other two. Add on the noise of battle and only the drummer himself would have been able to hear the beat, which would have defeated the object somewhat. High-pitched pipes or whistles were used to maintain rhythm since the higher the note the greater the degree of penetration.

Simply for the sake of imparting the information, the last time that galleys were used in a warfare situation was in the Baltic in 1809, during the Russo–Swedish War.

■ ■ ■

The friendly competition of a sporting 'round robin' somewhat masks the sinister origins of the expression.

To the monarchs and regional despots of early England, petitions of grievance were troublesome in the extreme in that they brought an ungainly and untimely halt to the day's pleasures. In an effort to dissuade the swinish multitude from cluttering up their palaces snivelling about starvation and other pri-vations that were their just desserts, it was customary to hold the threat of death over the first signatory to any petition considered unwarranted.

This did tend to make it a mite difficult to get petitions started (yes, I know this section is about shipping and the sea but, like British Rail, we're getting there) so the downtrodden got foxy and made a loop of paper or ribbon which they all signed and attached to the document making it impossible to identify the order of petitioners. The best-laid plans, and all that – the monarchs too got foxy and hanged the lot to make sure they got the right one.

In the British navy, (you see, I told you) the sailors used the same device when presenting petitions to the captain who, just like the kings of old, was entitled to hang the organiser on the grounds that his actions could be interpreted as inciting the crew to mutiny. Nevertheless by the time the English sailors had finished with the original French *rond ruban* – round ribbon – they had bastardised it to 'round robin'.

More often than not, with paper being in short supply to the crew, Navy round ribbons appeared with the signatures on the petition itself with the names appearing in the form of a cartwheel with spokes. Even this was far from foolproof. Captain Fitzgerald of HMS *Neptune*, obviously possessed of a malicious turn of wit, hanged all the men with names radiating from the hub of the wheel as he deemed them the 'spokesmen'.

The shift to sporting venues would appear occasioned by the fact that each participant in such a contest must at some time compete once with each of the others.

■ ■ ■

There is absolutely no connection between Satan and the expression 'between the devil and the deep blue sea' as used to describe an invidious situation with no visible means of escape.

On the hull of an old square-rigger the devil was a seam found just below the outboard decking which extended over the side of the ship, as if continuation of the main deck, thus providing a walk-way along the side of the hull. Anyone who found themselves between this devil and the deep blue briny would therefore be stuck on the side of the ship like a fly on the wall unable to board the ship because of the overhang of the outboard decking and with nothing below but a watery grave.

This same devil crops up in 'the devil to pay' which is invariably used in wholly the wrong context of 'there's been an almighty cock-up for which the devil will extract restitution.'

Not only is this devil a seam in a ship's hull but 'pay' has no connection with financial recompense since it is derived from the French verb *peier*, which means to daub or cover with hot pitch. The original and full expression, born in the shipyards of yester-year, was 'there's the devil to pay and no hot pitch' which demonstrates the expression's proper meaning of an awkward situation with no solution – until this devil was paid the ship was not seaworthy. In the shipyards the lowest seam near the keel was also called the devil and the ship would be even less seaworthy were this leaking.

How these two seams acquired their peculiar nickname is much debated, their awkwardness of access promoting the rather genteel theory that they were thus 'the very devil of a job to get at'. Given the colourful turn of phrase bandied about by sixteenth/ seventeenth-century sailors and shipyard workers, it is hard to imagine an exasperated Jack Tar turning to his fellow bilge rats and announcing with back of hand clamped to forehead, 'I say you chaps this bally seam is the devil of a job to get at.' Were this indeed the source of the name it is fairly sure that the seam would be called something that precluded its discussion here.

■ ■ ■

Although the press-gangs are still portrayed as illegal organisations that were tolerated they did in fact operate with the full backing of the crown.

Strangely enough, the word 'press' does not have any link with 'force', stemming instead from the now redundant 'prest', meaning lent, the ultimate source being the French *preter*, to lend. No contract can exist in English law lest there be financial consideration: in other words some money must change hands. When the new conscripts woke up aboard their new home they were given the Navy's equivalent of the Army's King's shilling, this being a few bob advanced out of their wages to seal their contract of 'enlistment'.

Nor is the reign of such gangs long over – the British Navy relied heavily on their activities until well into the nineteenth century. If you are in the habit of frequenting the water fronts and dock yards you would be well advised to keep your weather eye open for it is not yet illegal to press men into the Navy, although an act of 1835 stipulates that any man so forced must be released after five years service. What the hell – it's one way to see the world.

As trade opened up with the Far East, the abysmal conditions on board merchantmen dissuaded even the hardest sea dog from signing up to go China-side. Trading companies started pressing men hand over fist resulting in the most profitable port of call – Shanghai – donating its name to English to describe the kidnapping or spiriting away of a person.

■　■　■

In the old days a goodly percentage of a ship's crew – be it a merchantman or man-of-war – would have been made up of men rounded up by the press-gangs. A ship's captain making a call at port was reluctant to allow such men shore leave since they were bound to high-tail it leaving him exclaiming 'Look, no hands'! (Sorry, couldn't resist that.)

To keep this portion of his crew contented the captain would bring on board such entertainment as has long been the favourite of sailors on leave; many of these ladies chose to remain with the ship when it sailed. Indeed, one of the greatest scandals of the sixteenth and seventeenth-century Navy was the number of prostitutes that lived full time aboard men-of-war and not until the middle of the nineteenth century was the practice abolished in its entirety.

However, *revenons à nos moutons* – even if they do happen to be dressed up as lamb! In the morning when the boatswain entered the sleeping quarters to turn out the crew he would shout 'Show a leg or a purser's stocking!' This was the signal for those still a-hammock to hang a leg over the side. All the women were of course allowed to sleep on as they had been working the night shift, but if it was a hairy leg without a valid excuse at the other end, then the owner was unceremoniously turfed out on to the floor causing 'show a leg' to stand synonymous with 'get a move on'.

Given the hurly-burly and rough-and-tumble of below-decks life as shared by sailors and doxies it was of course a not infrequent occurrence for one of the latter to fall pregnant. If still on the high seas when her time came a makeshift canvas screen was slung between two of the midship guns to afford the girl some privacy during labour. This was the only place she could go without blocking a gangway which was, of course, far more important. Since paternity was at best a lottery and at worst pure conjecture the birth of any male child was listed in the ship's log as a 'son of a gun'. Female births were not considered worthy of mention.

■ ■ ■

Historically, the Navy has been the training ground for some of Britain's most prodigious drinkers, and one of the early free rum rations consisted of one pint of thick, incredibly strong rum per man per day. It is perhaps unnecessary to state that the vast proportion of England's sea force spent their entire time absolutely rat-legged, which is probably the only way they could tolerate the living conditions, the brutality of the onboard regime and the indescribable gore of close-quarter naval combat.

In 1740 along came Admiral Vernon, who decreed that the ration should henceforth be diluted, which did not go down at all well with the matelots now heavily into the DTs. Vernon was instantly recognisable by his highly distinctive boat cape made of a heavy material known as grogram, this earning him the nickname Old Grog which rapidly transferred to the new and unpopular ration in the reduced form of grog. All said and done it was still strong enough to make a man feel 'groggy'.

When a ship is heeled over hard in a storm it can happen that the sea can be breaking anything up to half way across the inclined decking. In such floundering circumstances the vessel is said to be 'half-seas over', her ungainly lurching turning this to a euphemism for drunkenness.

With typical perversity a sailor calls a rope a sheet, causing landlubbers much confusion; they naturally assume this to mean a sail. A square sail is secured at each base corner by one sheet, and when these are slackened right off they are said to be 'in the wind'. On a small craft this resulted in the loss of much of the drive causing the craft to lurch about at the mercy of the prevailing current and waves. Therefore, 'three sheets in the wind' is a sort of humorous intensification of this situation, alluding to a non-existent third sheet which if also slackened off could only worsen the situation.

■ ■ ■

Any prominent figure may find themselves referred to as the 'leading light' of their particular metier or organisation, but in the original maritime sense this did not mean leading in the sense of important but as in guiding.

At sea a leading light is a navigational aid which, when lined up with some prominent landmark, will lead a ship safely in to harbour or clear of some danger.

The seaman also uses 'make' to mean growing or increasing and as a landmark comes into view or becomes discernible through the fog it is said to 'make out' to sea. The expression has been hijacked by non-seafaring types who have turned it around as if it is the viewer who 'makes out' rather than that being viewed – 'I can't quite make out that sign over there', or whatever.

Also, when the sea starts cutting up rough with an ever-increasing swell which is obviously leading up to a storm it is then described as 'on the make', which has now moved into general speech to describe excessively ambitious people always on the look out for an opportunity and always trouble. The long and powerful undulations caused by distant storms are called the groundswell, hence this term's use to denote a low profile but very strong body of opinion which points the way or gives an indication of what is to come.

The term 'tidal wave' is a complete misnomer since these phenomena are anything but tidal in that they are caused by violent seismic disturbances on the sea-bed. In the open sea they rip along quite happily at around 600mph but maintain such a low profile that one would tear underneath a ship without the crew even detecting its passing. If nothing else, this shows up *The Poseidon Adventure* for the guff that it was as these killers only build up to such terrifying heights as they near shore. This they do in much the same way as any ordinary wave except that their incredible speed and power see them stack up to something approaching 300 feet when they hit land, still doing a few hundred miles per hour.

■ ■ ■

As every schoolboy knows, Captain Cook discovered Australia. But, as is so often the case, Macauley's ubiquitous schoolboy is wrong.

There is a distinctly racist attitude that creeps into reference books when they discuss the identity of a true discoverer of a land, for what they really mean is the first white man to get there. The Chinese knew all about Australia in the thirteenth century and discussed its existence with Marco Polo, who makes reference to such in his memoirs. For countless centuries the Malays were popping across to the north coast of Australia on hunting trips but, of course, they weren't European so they don't count either.

Even restricting ourselves to Europeans, Cook comes so far down the list that it is bordering on the farcical to use the word 'discovery' at all – even more so since he was actually sent there by an Admiralty cognisant of the continent's existence for almost a century.

The French and Portuguese have put forward the odd unsubstantiated claim of discovery in an attempt to grab some posthumous kudos on behalf of a variety of also-ran sixteenth-century explorers, but the 1605 sighting of the Australian mainland by de Torres is generally held to be the first. The first landing came a few months later in March 1606 when the Dutch ship *Duyfken* put ashore a foraging party at Cape Keerweer. So, by all the rules of the game, the otherwise undistinguished Captain Jansz of the *Duyfken* can claim to be the true discoverer of Australia. Throughout the next fifty years the Dutch were all over Australia charting and mapping their new toy, which was widely referred to as New Holland.

The first Englishman to start ferkling about Down Under was the pirate-navigator William Dampier, who turned up on the scene in 1688. Upon his return to England he reported his findings, which resulted in his being commissioned and packed off back to Australia in 1699 with instructions to have a good look round and report back. Dampier explored and charted some 900 miles of coast from Shark's Bay to Roebuck's Bay. Cook was ordered south by the Admiralty to observe the transit of Venus at Tahiti and then to proceed to Australia. Given all these facts it is a mystery indeed that Cook managed to grab all the limelight.

As for friend Dampier he was, by all accounts, a rude, arrogant, abrasive SOB who upset all and sundry. In 1703 he was a navigator aboard the privateer *Cinque Ports* on which sailed one Alexander Selkirk, the role model for Defoe's Robinson Crusoe. So unbearable did conditions on board *Cinque Ports* become that Selkirk demanded to put ashore at next land port which turned out to be the deserted island of Juan Fernandez. Here he languished for six years until rescued by the privateers *Duke* and *Duchess*. To quote the *Oxford Companion to Ships and Sea*:

'It says something of the state of discontent which had existed in the *Cinque Ports* that when Selkirk saw Dampier on board the *Duke* he asked to be set ashore again on Juan Fernandez.'

■   ■   ■

The Just and the Not-So-Just

The identity of the so-called Man in the Iron Mask has never been settled to anyone's satisfaction, but one thing is for sure, no matter how famous he was in fiction, he most certainly existed in reality. The only difference being that the mask he wore was of the finest velvet and the life he lived in prison was that of great luxury.

Whoever he was, the man was arrested the minute he landed at Dunkirk in 1669 by officials obviously aware of his return. The velvet mask he wore for the rest of his life was placed about his head, and they proceeded immediately to Paris. From here he was transferred to Pignerol, just outside Turin, then part of France. The instructions issued to his prison governor, one Monsieur St Mars, were as crystal clear as they were contradictory. He was to treat him with the greatest deference and see that his slightest whim for creature comfort was satisfied immediately irrespective of the cost – but, should he attempt to unmask himself or begin to discuss his true identity with his captors he was to be killed on the spot by any one of the two armed guardians who were to accompany him at all times to cope with such eventuality.

Nearly thirty years later St Mars was transferred to take over as Governor of the Bastille in 1698 and his charge was transferred along with him. Here the mystery man died to be buried under a false name in a grave that was guarded to prevent disinterrment.

Conjecture regarding the man's identity range from his being Louis XIV's double, his hitherto unknown older brother and thus rightful ruler, to a minor noble who was the King's rightful father after an adulterous liaison with Ann of Spain, but no one will ever know.

■ ■ ■

Despite the wide publicity American crime figures receive in the UK – hardly a week seems to go by without some report of a British tourist being gunned down on some city's streets within hours of arrival – the murder rates in America are far from the highest in the world. Despite the filling of one's fellow man with lead seemingly America's greatest participation sport, the annual statistics – both national and local – are surprisingly low.

Cape Town in South Africa regularly churns out figures dwarfing those recorded in New York and Chicago and when it comes to national overall figures the Brazilians really show us all up as a bunch of squeamish softies by streaking into the lead with an impressive 104 homicides per 100,000 population. This works out to about 370 murders for every day of the year which makes America, averaging between ten and eleven slayings per 100,000 population, look as if they simply aren't trying.

One of the most bandied about pieces of legal jargon is 'circumstantial evidence', almost consistently heard being employed to dismiss evidence that is weak, flimsy or deemed excessively flawed by coincidence. Indeed this very usage has engendered yet another myth that 'circumstantial' and 'coincidental' are synonymous.

Any evidence presented in a court of law which is not the basis of eye witness account is properly designated as circumstantial evidence – i.e. arising from the facts and circumstances of the case or crime. It is worth stating here that if there is one type of evidence that is notoriously contradictory it is that rendered by eye witnesses, all of whom can give a different account or interpretation of the same act.

Circumstantial evidence, on the other hand, includes the usually irrefutable forensic evidence (yes, I know this has taken a bit of a knocking of late) which can prove that the suspect was on the murder scene at the right time; that it was his skin and blood found under the victim's fingernails and that the victim was beaten to death with a blunt instrument later found in the suspect's home. All such concrete findings are properly termed circumstantial. 'Circumstantiate' is still used to mean corroborate and substantiate beyond any reasonable doubt.

It is a well established fact that the only people who rush off to join the French Foreign Legion are either hankering after lovers' amnesia or seeking sanctuary from the law. There may be the odd broken heart swelling the ranks of this famous/infamous force, but the Legion has never been the bolt hole of murderers and riff-raff, for what serious professional fighting body would want such recruits, and the Legion is nothing if not professional.

Founded in 1831 by Louis Phillipe, since when it has been in almost continuous action, the Legion does permit a man to assume a *nom de guerre* and to be referred to by such name at all times, but his true details must be recorded and all normal extradition laws apply. Being a Legionnaire has never placed a barrier between a culprit and the law.

So deeply entrenched is this myth that all applicants are screened by both Interpol and the Deuxième Bureau and only after they have been given a clean bill of health are they allowed to proceed and sign their five-year service contracts. Personally, I'd rather do a seven-to-ten stretch in the Scrubbs than five years in the Legion, but there you are. During the time between their application and background search being completed aspiring Beau Gestes are held as 'guests' of the Legion just in case they are wanted anywhere. As recently as 1984 two men were handed back to British police conducting a murder inquiry.

Another popular myth attached to the French Army is that when bestowing honours upon the rank and file, French Staff Officers always kiss the recipient on both cheeks. Not so. Officers only touch cheeks with the recipient in a gesture reminiscent of the dubbing of a sword to grant knighthood, but they never kiss them – well, not in public, at any rate.

■ ■ ■

Almost without doubt, some of the vilest criminals ever were those of the scrofulous brotherhood of pirates who were anything but the jolly, bluff chaps portrayed in adventure films. Nor did they ever fly a flag now called the Jolly Roger – they were not so honourable as to fly a flag announcing their trade to one and all thus giving the potential victim the chance to get in a couple of well-placed shots first.

In the early days most governments issued what were called Letters of Marque to any scum afloat who would take one. Basically this document permitted the holder to fly the flag of the issuing nation and plunder her enemies' shipping for a share of the proceeds. Thus the pirate could behave like a pirate but masquerade as a bona fide man-of-war and accrue all the protection accorded prisoners-of-war if caught.

Being a land-locked nation keen for a piece of the action, Austria issued Letters of Marque like confetti, resulting in a high proportion of the floating scum of the seas sailing under the Austrian flag, sporting a black double-headed spread eagle against a yellow background. It is arguable that at a distance this design could be fancied to resemble a skull and crossed bones and, indeed, the first hysterical ravings about such a flag did claim this colour scheme and not the now familiar black and white as favoured by the celluloid pirates of Hollywood. Either way, it is almost into the nineteenth century before the term is noted in print and would thus have been unknown to the likes of Morgan, Teach and co.

As to the origin of the name this does at least seem to have some foundation in reality. Known not only to privateers but also to regular ships of the line was a plain red flag which, if hoisted during an engagement, indicated a fight to the death with no quarter to be granted or expected. This was generally referred to as La Jolie Rouge and it seems more than likely that fact and fiction have somehow fused the two flags together.

■ ■ ■

Many the film in which some spy or other is shot full of a 'truth drug' and immediately rattles off everything he knows. What a load of old scopolamine!

Both lie detectors and the range of so-called truth drugs are extremely unreliable interrogation aids. The former monitor factors such as blood pressure, pulse and respiration rates and skin conductivity in an attempt to build up a stress profile of the subject and then identify lies. Anyone with a considerable amount of self control can and indeed has fooled such machines and a pathological liar who actually believes his own lies most certainly could.

As for the truth drugs, they are only as good as the interrogator. Once injected with scopolamine the subject descends rapidly into a twilight state in which they are highly suggestible and questioning could well induce confession through some deep-rooted guilt complex. Sometimes the subject agrees with everything the interrogator says in a childlike effort to please.

■ ■ ■

The origins of Scotland Yard go back a long way but it is fair to say that the British Police never held any offices at that address.

Back in the tenth century the kings of Scotland had to make an annual trip to London to pay homage to the English Crown and King Edgar, who ruled England from 959 to 975, presented the Scottish King Kenneth with a plot of land next to the Palace of Westminster so he could build himself a nice little des-res when down for his grovelling sessions. With the succession to the throne of James I of England – who was also James VI of Scotland – the necessity of such property disappeared and the buildings turned over to use as Government offices, having first been divided into Great Scotland Yard and Middle Scotland Yard. All of this took place in 1603.

It was the gentlemen of the nineteenth century press who were responsible for engendering the myth that there was a connection between Sir Robert Peel's new force and Scotland Yard. Peel set up shop in Whitehall Place (remember the old central police phone number – Whitehall 1212?) an address close to and accessible through Scotland Yard. Both the press and public latched onto the wrong address and used it as a collective term even though officialdom stubbornly continued to refer to Whitehall Place in all press releases and statements. In the end officialdom had to concede even to the extent of retaining it when the headquarters moved to new premises.

■ ■ ■

Legal anomalies abound; they always have abounded and doubtless always will. But nowhere do they more abound than within the confines of the House of Commons where the Members are completely unfettered by the laws that they themselves pass to constrain the rest of us.

Grouped together under the rather shadowy concept of Internal Affairs of the House (no, nothing to do with Pamella Bordes) Members can, amongst other things, run a brothel in the House, as indeed they may a casino. They may run an unlicensed still and traffic in the resultant booze, traffic in stolen goods, pornography, morphine and opium. They may acquire and carry unlicensed firearms, make bombs and fire explosive devices into the city from the Terrace in contravention of the Port of London Authority Act. The actual gunning down of an irksome constituent, who turned up to ruin all the fun by brandishing some petty grievance, would doubtless cause a few raised eyebrows but since arson and homicide within the House need not be justified such trivia would soon be forgotten. On the other hand, Members are not permitted to wear armour within the Chamber . . . well, there are limits. The last time these privileges were challenged was in 1935 with the case of 'Rex *v.* Sir R. F. Graham-Campbell, *ex parte* Herbert' – all privileges were upheld, so don't go hassling your MP!

At the time when whoever it was that shot President Kennedy fired the fatal shots in Dallas it was not a Federal offence to shoot the President of the United States, nor was genocide a crime under International Law when the Nazi war criminals were brought to trial at Nuremberg.

As a term, 'genocide' was the brain-child of Professor Raphael Lemkin of Duke University, Durham, North Carolina, and was invented expressly for the indictment. From a legal point of view genocide did not become a crime under International Law until 1948 when the United Nations passed a motion to that effect. This raised a difficult point at Nuremberg for at the time the Nazis had perpetrated their sick atrocities there was no such crime on the books so no one could be tried for it. Obviously, the events of the death camps could not be overlooked through such legal footwork but it would have been impossible to pick one name from the death-toll and go for murder by proving that all in the dock conspired to bring about the death of this one person. Thus a new charge had to be invented, causing some judges invited to sit at Nuremberg to decline since no one can be tried with retrospective legislation for 'new' crimes.

■ ■ ■

It is more than apposite that the term 'cheat' is derived from the activities of officers of the early Exchequer.

Back in medieval times the Escheators were officials of the Crown exchequer who were sent out to run properties and estates that had fallen forfeit to the

Crown through acts of treason or the inability of any heirs to qualify. The notorious and wholesale fiddling undertaken by this bunch of nest-featherers ensured the shortened form of their title would live long after their passing and stand as a monument to their unbelievable greed and corruption.

The modern title of Exchequer derives from a piece of chequered cloth – similar to a chess or checkers board – which was used as a calculating device. From the present state of the economy I think they must still be using it.

■ ■ ■

We are always hearing about American Grand Juries, but sixteenth-century England had them too. They gave us 'ignoramus' as applied to fools.

The Grand Jury of old would sit to study serious cases to decide if there were sufficient grounds to proceed for trial. If this was not the case they returned the indictment with 'ignoramus' written on the back. In legal circles this meant 'We take no notice of it' and prosecuting councils, peeved about having cases rejected, took it as an indication of the Jury's stupidity.

Although much conservative etymological opinion chooses to see the relationship between 'testify' and 'testicle' as remote, there is another theory backed up by much ancient tradition.

In the ancient courts it was not with hand on heart that one swore oath – castration being mandatory for bearing false witness. Not only did those bearing witness grip their own testicles and swear by their manhood but those swearing allegiance to a lord would be required to get a grip of his gonads whilst promising to be faithful and true. How unlike the life of our own dear Queen! This custom is referred to in the Bible in Genesis 24:2–3 which read 'And Abraham said unto his eldest servant of his house, that ruled over all that he had, Put, I pray thee, thy hand under my thigh; And I will make thee swear by the LORD, the God of heaven, and the God of the earth, that thou shalt not take a wife unto my son of the daughters of the Canaanites, among whom I dwell'.

In the Bible 'thigh' was a widely used euphemism for 'penis' as demonstrated by Numbers 5:21 '. . . the LORD doth make thy thigh to rot' and the old version of Genesis 8:30 claiming that 'Gideon had seventy sons going out of his thigh'. This would also explain why the Philistines were severely dis-chuffed after Samson had finished smiting them 'hip and thigh'.

■ ■ ■

The small pocket cosh or 'blackjack' strongly favoured by the not-so-just takes its name from the medieval taverns of Merrie England.

Life as a barmaid has not changed much over the centuries – there will always be those customers who presume that 'if she's working in a pub, then she must be available', but the tavern maids of old did have one defence against such dorks – their blackjacks. These were thick, heavy leather jugs that had been stiffened on the outside with tar and if someone really stepped out of line as the serving maids moved about the inn pouring out ale, these erstwhile Bet Lynches were not beyond issuing instant headaches by giving the unruly a good crack over the skull. These jugs were properly known as a gotch, so I suppose you could say that it would be a case of 'Gotcha!'.

As for the ladies who worked in the inns supplying bed and bawd, the designation 'hooker' has long been a popular tag which developed in nineteenth-century America. The first time it is noted it is being used in conjunction with the girls who worked the infamous waterfronts of Manhattan's Corlear's Hook but it required the proclivities of one of the more boisterous Union Generals to feature in the American Civil War to launch the term to a grateful nation.

General Joseph Hooker was once described by Charles Adams as 'A man of blemished character whose headquarters were a place that no self-respecting man liked to go and no decent woman could go, for it can only be described as a combination of bar-room and brothel.' On the other hand, it would appear that Hooker was uncommonly well liked by his own men and soldiers from other regiments demonstrated their touching affection for the man by constantly submitting transfer requests. One is forced to the conclusion that Hooker must also have been something of a tactical genius for, the inconvenience of the war permitting, other high-ranking officers never missed the chance to seek out his camp where they would while the night away discussing strategy.

With the massive concentration of troops around Washington at the time it was a natural development that the city's red light district would grow to ensure that supply met the constant demand. Almost over night this area of Washington became nicknamed 'Hooker's Division' and the individual whores-de-combat referred to as hookers. With the constant movement of troops in and out of the city the term spread like wildfire.

■ ■ ■

There is quite a big story behind 'titch' as applied to anything or anyone of diminutive stature.

The tale begins on 20 April 1854 when Sir Roger Tichborne, heir to the Tichborne estates and fortunes and all-round good egg, embarked on a ship bound out of Rio for Jamaica. Neither he nor the ship were ever seen again.

Back home in England old Lady Tichborne stoically and steadfastly refused to accept her son's death and immediately mounted a protracted campaign to find him by offering rewards around the globe for information. Apart from the inevitable crop of gold-diggers and con-men this produced nothing other than Tichborne being sighted more times than Lord Lucan. But, in 1866, by which time Lady Tichborne was well and truly ga-ga, there emerged from Australia a singularly repugnant confidence trickster who became known as the Tichborne Claimant. Among the innumerable glaring differences between the long lost son and the fat, tattooed, uncultivated slob who turned up was the fact that the claimant knew not a word of French, a language in which Tichborne had been fluent; at the time of his disappearance Tichborne had weighed an elegant nine stone and, Arthur Orton, as the con-man's name turned out to be, tipped the scales at a sweaty twenty-four stone and possessed all the finesse and social grace of an air-raid.

None of this mattered one jot to the dotty old girl who welcomed Orton with open cheque books and took him into her home. He immediately set about milking her for everything he could get and continued until her death after which the rest of the family moved in, secured Orton's arrest and after a trial which lasted 102 days and cost the family £90,000 even then, Orton was found guilty and banged up for fourteen years.

Born at the same time as the celebrated court case was one Harry Ralph who went on to become one of Britain's most successful music-hall comedians. A dwarf, he had at birth been not only extremely small but also extremely fat causing his parents to give him the nickname Tichborne. In the altered form of Titch or Little Titch, Ralph later used this as his stage name.

■　■　■

Fairgrounds and carnivals have long been favourite locations for those of the large dorsal fin to get their teeth into Joe Public's wallet. This was never truer than in medieval times when an old trick was to sell sucking pigs that weren't. The dupe would be shown a real live piglet in a sack which was promptly tied up again and put aside while the price was haggled over. When the deal was struck, the customer was given a different sack that actually contained a muted cat or puppy plus a bit of ballast. If the victim opened the sack before leaving the fair, he would literally 'let the cat out of the bag' and the game would be up.

This little bit of sharp practice also gave rise to 'being sold a pup' and 'buying a pig in a poke'. Poke, the diminutive of which is pocket, was once a common word for a small sack.

Yet another contribution to English phraseology from the fairground rip-off artists of yesterday is 'fast and loose'. As with 'find the lady' no one won at fast and loose, which was played with a leather strap and a metal skewer. The strap was doubled over, then rolled up and held fast, producing a loop at the middle. The sucker was given a skewer. When the shyster cried 'Loose!', he allowed the strap to unwind and the sucker had to stop it by arresting the loop with a single stab of his skewer. Try it sometime, it's impossible.

In Cambridgeshire, there used to be an annual fair on the Isle of Ely in the honour of St Audrey. Traditionally this was a market for some of the finest lace products but, perhaps inevitably, the fair became debased with cheap trash. 'Tawdry', a corrupted form of the saint's name, came to stand for such merchandise.

Every medicine man had a sycophantic assistant whose job it was to eat a piece of toad, then believed to be lethal so that the medicine's value could be 'proved'. 'Toad-eat' survives today as 'toady'. As one might expect the 'remedy' turned out to create more ills than it cured and whole villages were reduced to squabbling over the last dock leaves. Those members of the community mercifully unafflicted by Montezuma's revenge would set off in pursuit of the good doctor and force him to drink several bottles of his own brew – which, quite literally, gave rise to the expression 'a dose of your own medicine'.

'Kidder' first described faggots driven into loose soil or sand to bind it together but the word was hijacked by travelling men to describe the people they placed in a crowd to jolly things along and hold the audience. When the public got home with their purchases, they usually found out, too late, that they had been well and truly 'kidded'.

■　■　■

Have you ever wondered why we call a ship's hoist a derrick? Towards the end of the sixteenth century, a small fleet under the command of the Earl of Essex mounted an attack on the Spanish mainlands and sacked Cadiz. While ashore, officers and men – led by a Mr Derrick – picked up anything of value that was not nailed down and scurried back to their ships with booty aplenty for the English crown. In all the excitement some of the chaps forgot about a few little baubles secreted about their persons, a lapse of memory considered an act of treason by Essex, who had gone to Cadiz to rip off the Spaniards in the name of Queen and country, not private enterprise.

It was also suggested that these jolly Jack Tars had forced their unwelcome attentions upon the young ladies of Cadiz. Being a liberal-minded fellow, Essex decided the miscreants should be strung up, a sentence none too popular with the fleet which thought the activities of Mr Derrick and his pals fair game. There was a conspicuous lack of volunteers to carry out the hangings. With black humour, Derrick himself set about decorating the spars of Essex's flag ship with his own partners in crime. In recognition of his having lent a hand, his sentence was commuted to a flogging round the fleet, which in itself could amount to a death sentence but Derrick survived.

Tales of this charade spread across England and Derrick became something of a celebrity and capitalised on his new-found skills with the anodyne necklace by taking up the position of official hangman at Tyburn prison. His name soon became synonymous with the gibbet and, due to his previous exploits, the nickname spread to the hoisting device on ships as well as those on the dockside.

In an interesting side note to history, the wheel of fortune turned full circle for both Essex and Derrick for when the former was sentenced to death for conspiracy against the Crown in 1601 it was the latter whose job it was to nudge him into eternity.

■ ■ ■

Every country has a nickname (no pun intended) for the Black Maria: in parts of South Africa it is called 'mother's heart' because there is always room for one more.

The original Black Maria was one Maria Lee, a negress who was built like the proverbial brick outhouse and, in the late nineteenth century ran a boarding house in Boston not far from the central police station. Not being a lady to put up with any trouble and being possessed of arms like ham shanks, she was not beyond carting unruly tenants round to the police station and handing them over to the desk sergeant.

Having become a local character and had her exploits written up in the local papers, she soon became the subject of many cartoons. In these, the police were portrayed as being in difficulty and having to send for Maria Lee to help out. Before long her name became synonymous with the paddy wagon.

It is usually blackguards who are hauled away in a Black Maria and, although a slightly out-dated term, it nevertheless has an interesting history, too. The term came to life as a humorously bestowed title applied to the lowest of the low who spent their lives in the kitchens of sixteenth-century castles tending the fires, cleaning out the grates and scrubbing the pots. These, it must be remembered, were the days when cleanliness was only found next to godliness in an Irish dictionary and the members of the Black Guard would not have been the most fastidious members of the household.

Such mock military titles are still common today, members of various trades or professions being called the 'Whatever Brigade' or navvies labelled the 'Queen's Own Pick and Shovel' or 'McAlpine's Fusiliers'. In this case, the term 'blackguard' fell into disrepute because of the atrocious wages they were paid. You see, if they wanted any creature comforts they had to go moonlighting as footpads to pick up the wherewithal. Most people were of the belief that a blackguard would cut somebody's throat for the price of a pint. And they would not have been a million miles from right at that.

Religion and Rites

As far as the early Church was concerned the mentally handicapped were less than co-operative in that their very condition placed them, in the eyes of good compassionate Christians, beyond the salvation reserved exclusively for the sound of mind and body. Since it would have seemed a mite harsh to consign them straight to hell the Church found the solution in the invention of separate heavens and half-way houses, some of which live on in the realms of phraseology – e.g. 'fool's paradise'.

The next problem to receive the lofty attention of the theologians was that presented by all the stillborn babies, those who had died before they had a chance to be baptised and those who had lived and died before the coming of Christ. Yet again consignment to hell seemed inappropriate yet they could hardly be tolerated cluttering up the hallways to heaven. Ever ready with instant celestial plains, the Church hurriedly produced limbo.

This name they based on the ablative singular of the Latin *limbus*, a fringe or border, since it was thought proper that all such souls should jolly well hang around until the final judgement day so that the Boss could make the decision as to who went where.

This explains the use of 'being in limbo' but it could well be that the back-breaking dance also takes its name from the same source in that the body is held 'suspended' whilst the masochist contorts his or her way beneath the bar. Anyway, back to the Church and insanity.

Widely used is the expression 'a bit touched' to indicate someone not playing with a full deck, and this is derived from a rather more benign notion put forward by the Church who later saw idiots blessed in their ignorance and put in that state by the touch of the hand of God. Quite why the Church should chose to blame God is unclear but this nevertheless gave us the term 'cretin' which, believe it or not, is a simple variant of 'Christian'. Cretinism is a quite specific condition, the endemic form of which is found in the Pyrenees, causing the French to call such unfortunates *Chretiens*, which was simply their word for Christian.

■ ■ ■

Presuming that you accept the Bible's version of the so-called creation, there are several misconceptions attached to these two characters which have been perpetuated down the ages by artists and clergy alike.

First, let's look at the 'apple'. Genesis 3 simply refers to 'the fruit' and never gets more specific. That it was an apple is less than likely since Mesopotamia, where the Garden of Eden is traditionally held to have been, is far too hot for apple cultivation. The apricot is a good contender but the most likely fruit of the Tree of Knowledge is the fig, since it is only after having a nibble that Adam and Eve start rowing and sporting fig leaves to bury their differences. It was Aquila of Pontus who first started talking about apples when he translated the Song of Solomon from Hebrew into Greek. His choice of fruit was dictated by the fact that in his culture the apple symbolised desire and even lust. No one, and that includes St Jerome who translated the Old Testament into Latin, ever checked up, and the myth lived happily ever after.

Finally there is the belief that God gave Adam and Eve their marching orders out of anger at their having disobeyed his instructions to leave the Tree of Knowledge strictly alone. Actually, he drove them out 'lest he put forth his hand, and take also of the Tree of Life, and eat, and live for ever'. So it was divine concern at the prospect of man achieving immortality that prompted the eviction.

In fact, the example in Genesis of God telling Adam and Eve that consumption of the fruit would bring about their death when He knew full well it would do no such thing, is but one example in the Bible of God telling porkies, or getting others to go out and do his lying for him. For example Ezekiel 14:9: 'And if the prophet be deceived when he hath spoken a thing, I the Lord have deceived that prophet', or 1 Kings 22:23 'Now, therefore, behold, the Lord hath put a lying spirit in the mouth of all these thy prophets, and the Lord hath spoken evil concerning thee.'

Despite the much vaunted notion of Christians that there is but one God, the book of Genesis also casts a long shadow of doubt across this particular concept. Genesis 1:26, 'And God said, Let us make man in our Image' and Genesis 3:22 'And the Lord God said, Behold the man is become as one of us.' So, putting to one side the perhaps flippant suggestion that God was suffering from an Almighty multiple personality disorder, if prior to the Creation there was only God, then who on earth, or rather in heaven, was he chatting to?

■ ■ ■

There is a certain elitism that creeps into homicide in that those of elevated position are assassinated whilst the common herd have to be satisfied with being murdered. Just to digress for a minute, when those of frenzied temper are acused of 'screaming blue murder', this is taken from the French 'morbleu', itself a Gallic euphemism of 'mordieu', God's death. Anyway, back to assassins.

The original assassins were a bunch of drug-crazed Moslem fanatics who, in the eleventh century, rushed around slaughtering anyone opposed to their particular brand of the truth. So, it is rather fitting that the term was brought back to English by returning Crusaders coming home to rest from the fatigues of rushing round the same neck of the woods slaughtering anyone opposed to their particular brand of truth. God save us from those who know they are right.

As a word, 'assassin' is a corruption of 'hashshashin', or he who eats hashish, this being the drug the killers used to wind themselves up to fever pitch before embarking on some death-dealing sortie or other. The cult was started by a fanatic called Hassan ben Sabbah, nicknamed by the Christians The Old Man of the Mountain. Just as a matter of interest, Hassan was a classmate of Omar Khayam, no relation to the chap who was so impressed he bought the company. From his cave/fortress he sent forth his disciples to whom he was known as Ala-ad-din, the height of religion, a title surviving as Aladdin, a character to whom the cave still held great significance.

Another happily homicidal bunch were the Thugs, hence our use of the term. Widespread throughout India until the early nineteenth century, the Thugs believed that the more people they killed the better would be their reception by the Black Goddess, Kali. They infiltrated groups of travellers who were then ritualistically strangled in their sleep, this earning the Thugs their name from the Sanskrit 'sthag' – to hide or conceal. A close sister word is the 'thatch' which covers the roof so the surname of our dear ex-Leaderene, Maggie, somewhat appropriately means 'she who covers things up or conceals them'. She could also be a bit of a thug with her handbag.

■ ■ ■

On a more cheerful note, the Crusaders also brought back tales of St Nicholas of Bari upon whose shoulders the West was to build Santa Claus.

According to tradition, when not busy raising people from the dead, St Nicholas used to trundle around Asia Minor doing good deeds and saintly acts, one of which is commemorated today with the traditional Christmas stocking. It is told that Nicholas heard of three sisters who were to be sold into prostitution by their father because he was too poor to provide each with a dowry. To save the girls from this fate worse than death, Nicholas crept into their bedroom at night and dropped sufficient gold to constitute a dowry into each of the girls' stockings as they hung drying in front of the fire. It is, I suppose, too cynical to ask the obvious question of how come if they were so poor they each had stockings, a fire they could afford to keep burning all night in a house large enough to afford them a bedroom of their own? And, seeing as saints never boast of their good deeds and Nicholas obviously wanted to remain anonymous, how does anyone know he did this when the recipients were all asleep at the time? But enough!

As for the Christmas tree, for this we must thank St Boniface who popped across to Germany in the ninth century to teach the Teutonic hordes the error of their pagan ways. Boniface found the Hun heavily into worship of trees which they perceived as manifestations of the Earth's life force. Unable to break them of this irksome habit Boniface did what all early Christian missionaries did – absorbed the pagan ritual and then Christianised it. In fact, it is probably fair to say that there is not a single tradition, ritual, or festival that is original to the Christian faith.

To this end Boniface encouraged his ferocious flock to take small trees into their dwellings at Christmas time and to regard this as representative of the life force of Christ. This no doubt seemed like a jolly good wheeze to Boniface but it condemned the Western world to pick pine needles out of its carpets for eternity.

In Britain the Christmas tree was regarded as a nasty foreign habit which was vastly inferior to the kissing bough – a large globe of evergreen suspended from the ceiling. It was not until as late as 1848 when those trendy innovators Albert and Victoria –

both as German as get out — were pictured on the front of the *Illustrated London News*, gathered *en famille* round the Christmas tree, that the custom really caught on.

■ ■ ■

Still on the subject of Christmas, the modern image of Santa in his red-and-white costume parking his reindeer on the roof and coming into the house via the chimney is of relatively recent origin and has its ultimate source in the culture of the American Red Indian.

This image is taken wholesale from the well-known poem *The Night before Christmas*, written in 1822 by Clement Clarke Moore, an American professor of ancient languages. Initially intended purely for the entertainment of his own children, the story was published many years later, without his consent, in New York's *Troy Sentinel* and took America by storm.

Possessed of a passionate interest in ancient cultures, Moore was acutely aware that the American Indian was descended from Siberian stock who had simply wandered across into America when Russia was a continuation of Alaska. Moore looked to the Koryak tribesmen of Siberia for the foundations of this poem. The Koryak were, and still are, an almost stone-age civilisation entirely reliant on the reindeer for survival. In winter the Koryak go subterranean by digging massive rectangular pits, called yurts, which are topped by a ground-level birch-log roof. This is insulated by a covering of snow. A smoke hole is cut and is the only means of access.

A significant part is played in the Koryak culture by the hallucinogenic mushroom called the Fly Agaric, the most pronounced effect of which is a sensation of flight and disassociation with things terrestrial. Not only are the Koryak partial to blowing their minds but their reindeer will also eat any magic mushroom which they find. Nineteenth-century travellers to Siberia noted that the people were primitive but scrupulously honest and polite, the only danger being the risk of one's camp being trampled in the middle of the night by herds of hallucinating reindeer.

The spiritual well-being of the Koryak was overseen by itinerant shamans – a person reflected in the Red Indian witch-doctor or medicine man. These men were seen by the Koryak as communicators with the heavens and bringers of all bounties and gifts from the gods. To put himself in a 'spiritual' state, the shaman would pop a couple of magic mushrooms supplied by whoever he was visiting and the juice from the cooking and preparation was given to his reindeer. On a busy night the shaman got round quite a few yurts, both he and his reindeer getting progressively 'higher'. The reindeer and the shaman quite literally 'flew' along, the shaman would stop on the roof of his next point of call and fall in through the chimney.

Anyone with a question for the spirit world would ask the shaman to write it out on a piece of paper which was then burnt on the fire, the smoke acting as a communication channel to the spirit world. Using the smoke and the effects of the mushroom, the shaman would reach out with his mind for the answer to the questions and back through the chimney would bring the 'gifts' of messages from the gods. Even now, children still throw messages to Santa on the fire.

The popularity of Moore's poem led illustrator Thomas Nast to produce an illustrated version for a Christmas issue of *Harpers Illustrated Weekly* and his depiction of the jovial chap in a red-and-white costume – inspired by the red and white of the Fly Agaric mushroom – rapidly supplanted all previous images. So, if you hear mysterious fumblings on the roof one night soon, worry not, it's just a drug-crazed old Russian stumbling about with a sackful of goodies. Now that's what I call Glasnost!

■ ■ ■

One of the most deeply entrenched Biblical images is that of the animals gratefully marching two by two to join Captain Noah's Magical Mystery Tour. Unfortunately for this pleasant image, the Bible says otherwise. Genesis 7:2–13 states 'Of every clean beast thou shalt take to thee by sevens, the male and his female: and of beasts that are not clean by two, the male and his female. Of fowl also of the air by sevens, male and female, to keep seed alive upon the face of all the earth.' At the end of the day the whole story is palpably untrue – to flood the whole surface of the planet by raining for forty days and nights it would have to rain at a rate of just over fifteen feet per hour, and we all know it only rains like that in Manchester!

On the subject of beasts unclean, it would appear that the Jewish abstention from the eating of pork has no foundation in fear of trichinosis; to eat pig or boar was taboo because the animal had been the sacred totem of the early Hebrew people who venerated it. To quote Solomon Reinach: 'In the whole of the Bible there is not a single instance of an epidemic or individual malady attributed to the eating of unclean meats . . . To the Biblical writers, as to contemporary savages, illness is supernatural; it is an effect of the wrath of spirits. The pious Jew abstains from pork because his remote ancestors, five or six thousand years before our era, had the wild boar as their totem.'

Nor, it must be concluded from the Bible itself, did all Jews so abstain. Let's face it, as far as man is concerned a pig is not much use if not eaten; it gives no milk nor does it provide wool or anything else. So, who was keeping all these herds of Biblical swine that were forever tap-dancing on pearls and rushing head-long into lakes after being possessed by demons? Indeed, the ritual of driving sacrificial pigs into pits, as in the rites of Demeter and Astarte, is more than graphically reflected in that recount of the Gadarene swine.

To the Gentile mind, the most significant symbol of Judaism is the Star of David, yet it is only in the last hundred years or so that the symbol has held any great significance to the Jews. And as for it being called the Star of David, back in the days when David was giving the Philistines a hard time, the sign was completely unknown to the Jewish people. The hexagram was at this time revered in India where it represented the eternal sexual union between Kali and Shiva, the downward-pointing delta being female and the upward the male. This explains the rabbinical tradition that apart from the law tablets the Arc of the Covenant contains 'a man and a woman in intimate embrace, in the form of a hexagram'.

Whilst on the subject of David the giant-killer, it has to be said that 2 Samuel 21:19 originally stated that a chap called Elhanan bumped off Goliath, but to give David the honour instead some forger popped in the words 'the brother of' so the text now reads 'And there was again a battle in Gob with the Philistines, where Elhanan, a Bethlehemite, slew the brother of Goliath.'

■　■　■

Despite the widespread use of the insult, it is grossly unfair to take in vain the name of the noble Philistine and place it synonymous with the concept of an uncultured oik, for the Philistines were an extremely civilised Aegean people and if anyone deserves branding as uncivilised it was the Israelites.

In the twelfth century BC the Philistines settled on the coastal plain of Palestine and the Gaza strip and were quite happy until the Israelites turned up itching for a scrap and to turf the Philistines off their land. The very name of Palestine is a corruption of the name of the Philistines so things have not changed much in that neck of the woods over the last two thousand years or so. Anyway, the Israelites won the wars and got to write the history books, so the Philistines got all the bad press, but we have German student battles with the good citizens of Jena to thank for the modern connotations.

In that town in 1693 a bunch of Hooray Hermans from the university were sleeping off the excesses of the night in the hostelry wherein they had caroused. Taking advantage of the situation a gang of locals crept into the inn and beat to death a goodly number of the students as they lay in a stupor. Well, never look a gift-Horst in the mouth. For the sermon during the group funeral the university chaplain began with what he saw as the highly apposite text taken from Judges 16:12 which relates how Samson is attacked while asleep in Delilah's bedchamber and is awoken with the warning: 'The Philistines be upon thee, Samson.' From Jena the term spread like wildfire through academia wherein it was used to describe virtually anyone ouside such circles. Although the term was employed by the intellectual elite in England before the days of Matthew Arnold it was nevertheless he who gave 'Philistine' its wider currency through his writings in which he made much use of the term, most notably in *Culture and Anarchy* (1869).

Just one last thing about friend Samson – despite the countless paintings showing Delilah cutting off his lustrous locks with scissors, she did no such thing; according to the Bible Samson's head was shaved not shorn. Even so, it was not Delilah who performed the task but some Philistine who crept in and did the business while Samson slept. He must have been a jolly sound sleeper, that's all I can say.

■ ■ ■

Two of the most popular names for the Devil are Beelzebub and Lucifer, so it is something of a pity that neither name applies to Old Nick in any way, shape or form.

Beelzebub was actually a very important god of the ancient Israelites who had adopted the deity from, of all people, the Philistines to whom Baal-Zebub was the Lord of the Flies. Most ancient cultures perceived insects as psychopomps, or the embodiment of souls *en route* from this life to the next – in Greek *psyche* meant a butterfly.

As for the name Lucifer this appears but once in the Bible and does so in Isaiah 14:12–15, verses in which the alleged prophet is sniggering at the downfall of Babylon and the collapse of the reign of Nebuchadrezzar – yes, that is actually the correct spelling and not the '-nezzar' that is usually presented.

Nebuchadrezzar, you will remember, was he who had been 'weighted in the balance and found wanting' after the appearance of the mysterious 'writing on the wall' which informed him that he had had his lot. Never one to be backwards in coming forwards, the king had made some pretty strong boasts regarding his own supremacy to God and after his coming unstuck Isaiah uses the nickname Lucifer to take the mickey. The relevant passages read as follows: 'How art thou fallen from heaven, O Lucifer, son of the morning . . . For thou hast said in thine heart, I will ascend into heaven, I will exalt my throne above the stars of God . . . Yet [now] thou shalt be brought down to Hell.'

The name Lucifer basically means the light-bringer and, like all the female equivalents such as Lucille, Lucinda, Lucilla, etc. is built on the Latin *lux*, light. Isaiah is using the name to ridicule the king for saying he was going to make it up to the heaven and shine like a star. Whilst there is no prejudice in the Church against the christening of a girl with any of the aforementioned parallels, so deeply entrenched is the mistaken association 'twixt Satan and the name

Lucifer that it is a racing cert that a vicar would likely drown in the font any boy-child presented for christening as little Lucifer. Presumably this confusion is of relatively recent times since there was a famous fourth-century Bishop of Sardinia of such name who is still venerated as a saint on that island.

As to the reason for the confusion of these two unrelated personalities, this would appear to be based on yet another misconception – this being that Satan was kicked out of heaven for the sin of pride whereas he was booted out after losing a fight with Michael. Babylon – according to the Christians – fell as a result of the false pride of Nebuchadrezzar and it seems that this tenuous link was enough to produce the confusion.

Finally it is worth a deeper look at the aforementioned text from Isaiah since this is a classic example of whole chunks of the Bible being shamelessly plagiarised from earlier pagan writings. To the ancient Canaanites Shalem and Shaher were the equivalent of the Greeks' Dioscuri, and it is recounted that Shaher was secretly jealous of his brother the sun-god and made a take-over bid. The relevant text reads: 'How has thou fallen from heaven, Helel's son Shaher! Thou didst say in thy heart, I will ascend to heaven, above the circumpolar stars' etc. All of this was written nearly eight thousand years before the time of Nebuchadrezzar.

■ ■ ■

When it comes to the spider called the tarantula; the dance called the tarantella; the Italian town of Taranto; a peculiar condition one referred to as Tarantism and petulant children having a tantrum, there is an awful lot of confusion as to which term came first and which gave rise to the others. At the root of all these problems lies medieval Italian peasants tucking into good wholesome bread which turned out to be almost lethal.

It was far from uncommon in medieval times for entire communities to go doolally, claiming to be conversing with angels and enjoying regular visits from God and the Virgin Mary – but the cause was nothing more supernatural than ergot poisoning. This tended to strike entire communities after the bakers had produced bread made from contaminated rye. Not only is ergot a prime source of LSD but it also induces muscular spasm and delirium characterised by 'visions' of a pseudo-religious nature. Needless to say, the Church preferred to see this as a miracle and dismiss any deaths as the unfaithful unable to accept the visitations.

In the Italian town of Taranto outbreaks of such hysteria began happening with such monotonous regularity that the unkind might suggest that the locals were hamming it up to maintain the flow of tourists and clerics who came to witness the incidents. Composers began writing lively dance pieces reminiscent of the peasants' cavortings and so called them tarantellas. As for the spider, this abounded in the region of Taranto and the town's fame/infamy caused 'tarantula' to become something of a blanket term for big, hairy spiders.

Originally the term 'tantrum' described a child's spinning top which had a built in eccentricity resulting in the damn thing flying all over the shop crashing into things like one of the possessed peasants. The top was hurled out of a loop of twine and it was not long before 'throwing a tantrum' shifted in application to the child in such a mood. The more modern 'throwing a wobbler' is likely a spin-off – no pun intended.

The association between delirium and the influence of the gods was widespread, hence 'giddy' being an old English word for god-possessed. The priests would encourage the flock to hurl themselves about à la whirling dervish and the sensation of dizziness would be explained as the effect of the gods entering the body.

As a matter of interest, the last recorded outbreak of ergot poisoning occurred in the French town of Pont-Saint-Esprit in 1951 when the locals exhibited all the classic symptoms and there were even a few deaths.

■ ■ ■

Some of the older confessional boxes still sport carved designs of the rose, which is intended to indicate that anything said within is in the strictest confidence or, *sub rosa*, under the rose. As to why the rose became the symbol of confidentiality, for that we must look to Greek mythology.

The story goes that Venus was engaged in some pretty serious horizontal jogging with a minor deity who had taken her fancy when she was caught red-handed – well, red-everythinged, in fact – by Harpocrates, the god of silence. Harpocrates was making strong hints that he might not live up to his title when along trotted Cupid, the gross little product of Venus's previous dalliance with Mercury. Never venturing far without the tools of his dubious trade, the troublesome toxophilite proffered Harpocrates his special red rose that never wilted. One cannot help thinking that Harpocrates could have held out for a better deal for his silence, but there you are. As a result of the yarn the ceilings of Court antechambers and the like were traditionally decorated with roses to remind all below that the discussions held were, quite literally, *sub rosa*.

The modern image of Cupid is invariably that of a cherub, but in the old days Cupid was otherwise perceived and a cherub is properly a pretty ugly creature of man's darkest imagination. Basically winged monsters of bestial aspect, the cherub was something straight out of a pagan nightmare but was nevertheless adopted into the culture of the early Christians. Much later, artists trying to please the Church deliberately misrepresented the cherub by making it the twee little brat that has fluttered across a thousand canvases.

Cupid is now seen as a bowdlerised cherub capable of firing an arrow that runs unerring to its target in the heart, but he was initially represented as a winged phallus which ran just as unerring to its own target. This will explain why in modern Italy *ucello* can still mean either a small bird or that same appendage. The Roman counterpart of Cupid was Eros, he suffering similar whitewashing. But it is wrong to call the famous statue in London's Picadilly by his name. The monument was erected in tribute to the philanthropy of the seventh Earl of Shaftesbury in 1885, the year of his death. The piece was entitled The Angel of Christian Charity and was intended to personify Christian love, not the more earthy kind.

■ ■ ■

The number of references to Thomas à Becket vastly outnumber the proper form of plain old Thomas Becket. Although born in London, Becket was the son of Norman merchants, but the family name was never 'à Becket', this form being a mickey-taking nickname used by his detractors, but never to his face. There is not a single written contemporary reference to the man under such name. As for the story that his murder was instigated by Henry II's exasperated cry to be rid of 'this turbulent priest', this simply does not ring true. Far more likely is that the rash monarch put out a contract on Becket which was subsequently bungled by the four knights who popped down to Canterbury to put the hit on the Archbishop. Only after court involvement was palpably evident did Henry get into the old wailing and gnashing of teeth in regret for his supposed intolerant outburst.

Anyway, no matter – Canterbury became a point of pilgrimage which was jolly good for business for the local clerics and monks who started churning out tourist tat and selling forgiveness in the form of certificates of indulgence. You could even sin on the never-never by buying indulgences in advance for misdemeanours you might want to commit in the future. The easy pace set by the mounted pilgrims on their journey from London produced the term 'Canterbury gallop' this now surviving as the elliptic 'canter'.

The well-dressed pilgrim also bedecked himself and his mount's harness with little bells to frighten away evil spirits. This too was the original purpose of Church bells, only later did their sound come to be regarded as a summoning of the faithful. The flower now called the Canterbury bell was fancied to resemble in shape the pilgrims' bells.

In the medieval era pilgrimages were all the rage and Europe literally teemed with peregrinatory faithful *en route* from one shrine to another. Naturally, the biggie was Rome and if you were going to take the trouble to go that far you might as well first plan a route that would take in the maximum number of points of worship on the way. The circuitous meanderings that this involved caused the name of the final destination to describe such wanderings and the spelling gradually changed to 'roam'.

Every good pilgrim-about-town needed a good, hardy cloak to keep him as comfortable as possible whilst on the road. The French came up with the answer in the form of a new hard-wearing material they called *gauvardine*, their word for a pilgrimage. Today the cloth is called gabardine and still makes the macs hated by all good schoolchildren. And, talking of children and pilgrimages, that leads nicely on to the Pied Piper of Hamlin.

The year 1212 saw in Europe an extraordinary phenomenon resulting in children leaving home in their droves to join what became known as The Children's Crusade. Under the leadership of a boy called Nicholas, some 50–60,000 German children set off over the Alps to Rome and another 40,000-odd quit France under the guidance of Stephen of Cloyes. Pope Innocent III went out to meet the leaders and the survivors of the journey and basically told them to naff off home because they certainly were not wanted in Italy. They drifted to the ports where they found no shortage of ship's captains only too willing to give them free passage home – only they never got there. The boats sailed directly for North Africa where the children were sold to the Moslem slave markets. None of them was ever seen again.

■ ■ ■

In the halcyon days before Mr Arnold met Mr Chipendale and blended their names to give Arndale Centres to a grateful public, all traders were itinerant, moving round in wagons chasing up the trade. All, that is, except one type of trader, the purveyor of pens and paper.

In such times the Church held the stranglehold on the scribing trade and few outside the clergy could read or write. So, if you wanted to send a letter, you had to pop round to the local church or monastery to have it written and the recipient had to do likewise to have the contents revealed to him. Yes, you are right, a scribe with a malicious turn of wit could have had a ball. Anyway, it was not long before dealers in such goods set up permanent shops in or near Cathedrals and the like, and the first fixed shops were called stationary stores!

As for the traders on the road, they needed assistants to show the goods off to the best advantage to the crowd, which really boiled down to holding them up in the air. As all trades took to fixed premises these assistants took on duties more akin to window dressers, usually setting off the merchandise against a pleasing backdrop of cloth. Their original title of upholderers transmuted to 'upholsterers' and their work with cloth became more and more specialised.

Getting back to the clerical scribe – their monopoly of old still reflected in terms such as 'clerical' in the office sense – it is well to look at the influence of the Vatican scribes who used a particular script, hence 'italics'. Now then, if there was one thing for which the Vatican was rightly famous it was murder and treachery and, although the expression is not so often heard these days, talk of seeing someone's 'fine Italian hand' in some plan or other is still understood to mean the obvious touch of a particular person's treachery.

When the Popes were not busy breaking every commandment in the book, they were usually busy breaking their solemn vows of chastity – one Pope was actually beaten to death when caught discussing Uganda with someone's wife. But, when it comes to Papal debauchery, the Borgias take the biscuit. Rodrigo Borgia died after absent mindedly drinking wine he had poisoned to bump off some irksome Bishop, and the only mystery surrounding the infamous Infanta Romana as produced by Lucrezia Borgia was the identity of the father – was it her father Rodrigo or her brother, Cesare.

Not unnaturally all this chastity practised by the Popes produced countless off-spring who could not be openly acknowledged as their sons and heirs – girls were simply hived off to eager nunneries thus sure of Papal patronage, of the financial type for a change. When such lads grew up and began to move in Vatican circles the accepted nicety to explain their favour in the eyes of the Pope was to hail them as his nephews. From the Latin *nepos*, a nephew, we derive 'nepotism' which still describes unfair favour given within an organisation to family of the leaders.

■　■　■

Those bent on extracting a terrible revenge or imposing draconian measures are fond of justifying their actions by 'quoting' the Biblical 'vengeance is mine, sayeth the Lord', or 'an eye for an eye' etc. Unfortunately for those who favour the first sentiment, the relevant passage in Romans 12:19 reads: 'Dearly beloved, avenge not yourselves, but rather give place unto wrath: for it is written, Vengeance is mine; I will repay, saith the Lord.' As for the second justification this is part of the Lex Talonis which was instituted to prevent the very actions intended by those who incorrectly invoked the sentiment. Far from meaning that people should go around ripping out others' eyes and teeth, the law was intended to make the punishment fit the crime – to the letter. The legislators were only too well aware that excessive response only created a self-exacerbating spiral of feud.

No two pieces of Christian dogma are more misunderstood than those relating to Original Sin and the Immaculate Conception. It is probably a fair bet that 999 out of 1,000 people would tell you that man's original sin was sex, but it was actually disobedience. The boss told Adam and Eve not to eat of the fruit but they went ahead and did it anyway. As for the Immaculate Conception, it is probably also fair to say that the same 999 people will tell you with supreme confidence that this relates to the supposed miracle of the Virgin Birth. Wrong again.

Having invented the notion of Original Sin the Church further decreed that all were tainted with the same brush since Original Sin was contracted in the womb like some virus and all 'born of woman' were inescapably marked for life. Now then, this was fine until with much nervous and tentative clearing of throat someone chose to remind the orthodoxy just who else was 'born of woman'. To avoid the embarrassment of trying to market a sinful god the Church had to do some quick thinking and squared away any awkward questions by inventing the Immaculate Conception. Not being defined as 'of faith' until 8 December 1854, this was a sort of backdated honour bestowed on Mary to render her clean of Original Sin so that she would then be 'clean' enough to carry the Christ without transmitting to him some awful disease. So, the Immaculate Conception refers to the conception of Mary within the womb of her mother.

No matter how popular the Madonna/Whore syndrome so vigorously marketed by the early Church, there is not a single biblical reference to the other Mary following the oldest profession. The Christian patriarchs chose to brand her a whore and that was that.

■　■　■

The letters IHS are popularly, yet incorrectly, believed to represent any one of the following: *Iesus Hominum Salvator* (Jesus, Saviour of men); or *In Hoc Signo* (In this sign [you will conquer]); or *In Hac Salus* (Safety in this [the cross]).

IHS is nothing more than the abbreviated form of the Greek equivalent of the name Jesus, which is Iesous, IHS being but the first two and last letters. It is obvious that there is a double misconception here; the 'H' is not an 'H' at all but the long Greek 'E' which just happens to be represented by the symbol 'H'. This was mistaken by those people familiar with the Latin culture, but ignorant of the Greek, as being the letter 'H'. Because of this, IES might be better but, either way, the frequently seen form of IHS makes no more sense than does putting JIM instead of 'James'.

■ ■ ■

Every year thousands of schools throughout the world put on Nativity plays which go a long way to perpetuate some of the most deeply entrenched myths in the Christian tradition of the visit of the Magi.

For a start there is not a single indication that the men making up the delegation held the rank of king and secondly, no one knows how many there were because Matthew neglects to say. In the second century the theologian Origen pronounced off his own bat that the number of dignitaries had been three. He was presumably working on the basis that there had only been three different types of gift but there's nothing to say that any number of men within the delegation didn't turn up bearing gold for example. By the sixth century, a great deal more importance had been placed on the visit of the Magi – that being the title of an ancient priestly caste of Persia. Bede decided that they really ought to be more elevated, so he not only promoted them to kingship, but he also bestowed the now traditional fancy names of Melchior, Caspar and Balthazar.

Next we have the romantic image of the three kindly old monarchs following a guiding star across the desert to the stable in Bethlehem. Not according to the Bible we haven't! Matthew tells us that the Magi saw a heavenly body rise in the east, which prompted them to travel west to Jerusalem – hardly following at all. Upon their arrival in that city, they went straight to the court of Herod to inquire where the Christ was supposed to be born. After consulting his prophets, the King told them to go to Bethlehem, and it was on the last leg of the journey that they supposedly held the star in sight, but, since they were already well aware of their destination it is quite fair to say that they did not actually follow the star at any point in their journey. At the risk of over-egging the pudding, it is also fair to say that, had a star come so close to the earth as to identify an individual dwelling, then not only would the occupants be incinerated but so too would the entire middle east prior to the earth being thrown out of orbit which would rather render the First Coming something of a redundancy.

Innumerable religious paintings and countless Nativity plays have compounded into longevity the error that the Magi visited the 'stable' immediately after the birth. Only the shepherds turned up at the birth scene; the Magi visited the 'young child' Jesus in 'the house' and, if anything in the Bible can be regarded as historically or chronologically accurate, there must have been a gap of at least two years between the two events because of Herod supposedly ordering the death of all children up to the age of two after the Magi had passed through his court.

Either way, the Church recognises the events as being wholly separate which is why they celebrate the visitation by the Magi with Epiphany on 6 January.

■   ■   ■

There is not a single, reliable Biblical source to confirm that Jesus Christ was born in a stable in Bethlehem on 25 December 1BC. Come to that there isn't a single corroboration to such assertion to be found in any written text. In fact the whole concept and image of the birth of Jesus is one of pure Western fantasy and invention.

It is only in the now-accepted versions of the Gospels attributed to Matthew and Luke that we get any mention of the time, place and manner of the event – Mark and John avoid the issue completely, which is significant in itself. Almost universally recognised as having been written around a century after the events that they describe, and clumsily attached to the front of the Gospels concerned, the two conflicting accounts of the Nativity are not only highly contradictory, but are at best extremely shaky and full of holes, and at the worst pure fabrication. This latter does seem to be the most likely of the two possibilities. Jesus is known to have grown up in Nazareth and there is no earthly reason why he shouldn't have been born there as well. There were, however, unearthly reasons for the birth to be moved to Bethlehem and, because the old prophecies foretold that the Messiah would be born in Bethlehem, whoever it was that revamped Matthew and Luke turned history on its head to contrive the birth to have taken place in Bethlehem and thus corroborate and reaffirm Jesus's credibility as the Christ.

According to Matthew, Jesus's parents were resident in Bethlehem in a house at the time of the delivery and, in so far as the circumstances and physical surroundings are concerned, he reports nothing unusual. Matthew (we shall call him that for the sake of argument and extend the same privilege to Luke) now has a problem in that he has to get the family back to Nazareth where they really belong. This he achieves, via Egypt, by the invention of the so-called Slaughter of the Innocents by Herod, and by having Joseph forewarned of the grisly event by a heaven-sent dream. Matthew would appear to be the only person who considered this incredible act of wholesale infanticide worthy of mention. It is not mentioned anywhere else in the Bible and there is not a scrap of corroborative evidence to back it up. In short, it simply didn't happen. Matthew most likely got the idea from the story of the Pharaoh who put all the Hebrew first born to the sword.

Luke is even more inventive in his attempt to place the birth in the desired place. He tells us that Joseph and Mary lived in Nazareth but that, while Mary was pregnant, they had to go to Bethlehem to be counted in the Roman census being organised by Cyrenius. Everyone, Luke tells us, had to return to the city of his lineage to be counted. Joseph was of the House of David, Bethlehem was the City of David – ergo, Joseph and Mary must go to Bethlehem. Now, this may well sound very plausible, but if there is one thing known about Roman-census taking methods it was that everyone stayed put, kept travelling to a minimum and waited for the officials to get round to them. Can you imagine the chaos caused by half the country suddenly going walkabout the length and breadth of the nation, not to mention whole family groups having to abandon their farms, crops, homes and livestock for weeks on end while they trekked off to some distant city. Nazareth to Bethlehem, for example, is some eighty-odd miles. So, did they live in Bethlehem and escape to Nazareth or did they live in Nazareth and go to Bethlehem? It can't be both. Most strikingly of all, the Cyrenius census is known to have taken place in the year AD6 and Herod is known to have died in 4BC. To put it bluntly, both are lying and the most disturbing thing about that is the question as to why they should feel the need to do so in the first place. Why not just ignore the whole question as did the other two gospels.

It is, to say the least, extraordinary that when it comes to the most talked about and significant figure in Western culture, nobody knows where he was born, when he was born, or even when he died. This has not stopped the speculation. Various astronomers through the ages have tried to pin-point the year by linking it to the occurrence of known celestial phenomena – not least of all Halley's comet. Such speculation is all very well, but such an approach to the question presupposes the existence of the so-called Star of Bethlehem, and we only have Matthew's very shaky word for that.

The first mention of Christmas being celebrated on the now traditional date appears in the Philocalian Calendar which cites the year 336. It was over a century later, in 440, when the Church finally fixed the date for Christmas. There was no Christian motivation for the choice of 25 December, rather the opposite since they pitched the ceremony to coincide with two of the most significant pagan ceremonies, the Yule of Northern Europe and the Roman Dies Natalis Invicti Solis (Birthday of the Unconquered Sun). The early Church always found it easier to adulterate and adopt, or simply blend in with existing pagan practice rather than attempt to eradicate it.

Probably fixed for all time is the image of Jesus being born in a stable, all warm and snugged up with the animals. Again, this is but Western invention left unsupported by a scrap of biblical foundation. The Luke account simply states that whilst in Bethlehem 'the days were accomplished that she should be delivered'. Which is hardly the last-minute, abdomen-clutching dash across the desert as fixed in the Western imagination. Also, the original Greek version of Luke places the birth in a *katalemma*, this denoting any temporary shelter or a cave. Early Christian tradition certainly places the event in a cave and it was over a cave that Constantine built the Bethlehem Church of the Nativity. Luke also located the Last Supper in a *katalemma* but no one has so far come forward with the suggestion that Jesus and the disciples got together in a stable for a meal.

■ ■ ■

Fundamental to so much of the Christian faith is the belief in the Virgin Birth, but this was not a notion that reared its head until about a century or so into time AD. And to put it bluntly, the early Christians demanded their god be formed of such process, not through some fastidious avoidance of nasty, earthy sex, but because everyone else seemed to have gods produced by parthenogenesis, to give the procedure its fancy name.

A quick glance at the mythologies of old will reveal that virgin births were ten a penny; widespread throughout the ancient world was the belief in mortal women impregnated by gods and the Christians wanted a piece of the action. Even Genesis 6:4 talks of giants walking the earth because 'the sons of God came in unto the daughters of men, and they bare children to them'. Everyone from Perseus to Plato was born of a virgin mother so someone had to go back to the scriptures and indulge in a little careful 'interpretation', I think they like to call it. Basically, they took the Hebrew *almah*, which simply means young woman, and 'translated' this into the Greek *parthenos* which can only denote a woman who is virgin in the purely physical sense.

The main trouble with such deliberate forgery is the inconsistency it leaves behind. For example, those who place much store by the concept of the ever-virgin Mary find uncomfortable the references to Jesus as Mary's 'firstborn' as indeed they do with biblical reference to his four brothers – James, Joses, Simeon and Jude, and two sisters, names unknown.

As a word 'virgin' hides something of an insult to all women. The term is rooted in the Latin *vir*, man, and basically means a woman lacking a man. Similarly, only a man can have 'virtue'; only a man can acquire sufficient skill to become a 'virtuoso', and, best of all, a 'virago' is, etymologically speaking, a brave and heroic woman who is almost good enough to be a man. Don't tell the publishing company.

■ ■ ■

At the risk of sounding a real party-pooper, nor was Jesus nailed to the cross in the manner so widely depicted; in fact we cannot even rely on the Bible for clear statements that Jesus was attached to a cross of any description.

Here again the Bible argues with itself and despite the claim made by John at 19:35 that his account of events is 'vouched for by an eyewitness whose evidence can be trusted' not one of the crucifixion accounts can possibly have been written by anyone contemporary to the alleged event. John's account states that Jesus carried his own cross all the way to the killing ground and Mark says that Simon of Cyrene did it for him. Acts repeatedly states Jesus to have been killed and hanged in a tree (Acts 5:30, 10:39 and 13:29) and 1 Peter 3:24 informs us of a similar fate. Unfortunately, Galatians 3:13 states that 'Cursed is everyone that hangeth on a tree.'

Accepting for a moment that a cross was involved, nowhere in the Bible is there mention of nail wounds in the feet. Only in John's 'eyewitness account', is there mention of nail wounds at all, these being in the hands. This is yet further proof of the invalidity of John's word since no one was ever nailed through the hands for, as a moment's thought will show, any such fixing would simply tear straight through under the victim's own weight. Roman execution procedure is well documented and the nails – if used at all for they were quite unnecessary to the procedure – were driven in through the wrist. The officer in charge had to watch for the involuntary clench of the fist which indicated the nail had penetrated the median nerve and if this reaction was not forthcoming, then the nail was retracted and driven in again. Charming, but one is nevertheless moved to ask why those individuals claiming to be marked with the stigmata are always sporting the wounds in the wrong place.

As stated, nails were both expensive and unnecessary since the cause of death on the cross is suffocation and not as is widely imagined, shock, loss of blood or whatever. After hanging by the arms for a short time, violent cramps beset the chest making breathing difficult as a result of pressure on the diaphragm. This can only be alleviated by the victim alternating the weight from arms to legs until, too tired to continue, they slump and rapidly die of asphyxia.

With good reason, the early Church did not think the crucifix a wizzo marketing ploy guaranteed to bring in countless converts so they played it down for quite a time. Not until the ninth or tenth century did this come out of the closet by which time artists got the details wrong. The stigmata bunch made their mistake by taking their lead from artists' impressions instead of doing their homework.

■ ■ ■

Miscellanea One

The history books are constantly accusing Walpole of being this country's first prime minister. Not only is this an impossibility by some 200-odd years but had you so addressed Walpole or any of his immediate successors, you would have found yourself fighting a duel.

In Walpole's day and for quite some time after 'prime minister' was a political insult levelled at leaders of the House of Commons who were no more than the mouthpiece of an unpopular monarch willing to appoint to ministerial office whomsoever the Crown wanted. In effect, this would boil down to a Cabinet of yes men. You see, it was not long after the days when the king himself was the supreme political figure, that is, the first or prime minister – 'L'Etat, c'est moi', and all that jazz.

Since the office of prime minister did not even officially exist until 1937, Stanley Baldwin can rightly claim to be the first British prime minister. Despite this official recognition of the title, the plaque outside Number 10 Downing Street still announces to the world that it is the residence of the First Lord of the Treasury, that being the proper title prior to 1937. Including John Major we have so far had fifty 'prime ministers', thirty-seven of which have been public schoolboys (excluding Mrs Thatcher), Eton and Harrow accounting for twenty-five. A total of thirty-eight studied at Oxford or Cambridge, which would seem to indicate a slight class bias in the office.

In the late 1880s, Robert Gascoyne-Cecil, third Marquess of Salisbury, had his hand on the country's rudder. In what appeared to be blatant nepotism to some, he appointed his nephew, Arthur Balfour, to a series of the best jobs. Those jealous of his connections said that Balfour only had to hint that he fancied some ministerial post or other and it would be his, just like that, this likely giving rise to 'Bob's your uncle' as said of anything easy of acquisition.

Can you think of a famous British prime minister who was part Red Indian? Although a difficult man to scalp, Winston Churchill was part Iroquois; his mother, the outrageous American-born Jenny having had a great grandmother who was a full blooded Red Indian squaw.

Talking of Westminster, did you know that Westminster Abbey is not in fact an abbey and has not been since the times of Henry VIII and the Dissolution of the Monasteries. This stands as a truth if for no other reason than that there has not been an abbot in residence since such time. Since 1560, the official title of the building has been Collegiate Church of St Peter in Westminster.

■　■　■

'Claptrap' started out as theatre jargon to describe any gambit or strategy calculated to elicit applause for absolutely nothing. The idea behind this was that if you built enough clap traps into a shoddy act, the audience would sit barking with laughter and clapping like a bunch of sycophantic seals. Afterwards, they would walk out thinking that they had seen a great show.

The best example of a modern clap trap is the one that invariably appears in all downmarket magic acts. When the chap on stage needs some prop or other, out staggers a scantily clad blonde whose bombshell exploded years ago to hand him a hat with the rabbit hidden inside, or whatever, before turning to the audience to hold out her arms as if she had just performed some earth-shattering feat. The crowd obediently applaud – it never fails.

■ ■ ■

In 1652, Peter Stuyvesant was worried about attacks by hostile Indians and the possibility of New Amsterdam being invaded by the British, so he built a massive stockade wall to protect the settlement that was to become New York. When banking and finance later became organised, the profession occupied the street where the wall had once stood – hence Wall Street.

New York's infamous Bowery stands on the land that once was Stuyvesant's farm. Its name derives from the Dutch for a farm or dwelling, *bouwerij*. The South African Boer's name derives from the same word and the term also crops up in English in the word 'neighbour' – the nearest farm.

When early neighbours fell out, it was usually over

water rights, which is why 'rival' derives from *rivus*, the Latin for a river or a stream.

■ ■ ■

After months on the trail, where the only females had horns and halitosis, the average trail-hand was not going to be satisfied with a sarsaparilla and a Book at Bedtime when he hit town. Having got paid, it was straight over to the red-light section to pick up the local culture and get good and sozzled before shooting up the town.

Western towns were not as large as you might imagine, so it did not take too many drunken cowhands, accompanied by the ladies of their choice, to spread red-light behaviour to sections of the community where it was less than welcome. The expression 'painting the town red' developed in such railhead towns as Abilene, where every night was Saturday night.

■ ■ ■

As a term for a massive lorry 'juggernaut' is a corruption of the name Jagannath, one of the Krishna reincarnations of Vishnu. Traditionally, a massive idol of the god is dragged through the streets of Puri in Eastern India, to transfer the god to his summer residence. A cart of staggering proportions is used for the purpose – hence our usage.

A myth has grown up that the demented faithful tossed themselves under the wheels to be crushed to death and thus released from the unending cycle of life and rebirth. There have been deaths over the years, but these have mainly resulted from crowd pressure rather than by fanatics electing to rush rudely unannounced into the presence of their creator.

■ ■ ■

No book of unsolved mysteries is complete without various 'authenticated' reports of torrential downpours of fish, frogs, worms and all sorts cascading from the heavens onto the heads of surprised people. Surprised! Half dead, more likely. Being hit on the head by, shall we say, a ten-pound fish – for many of the reports have cited downpours of fish of this size – is not going to do anyone a great deal of good. Since fish are possessed of a perfectly aerodynamically shaped body they are going to have a terminal velocity of something in the region of 250mph and believe me, that would do more than ruffle your hair. The same reports often claim that the fish were flapping about on the ground after landing, which is surprising to say the least, for they are going to have more than a mild headache themselves.

In recent times, reports of such occurrences have been conspicuously lacking in the richer countries which have advanced communications capable of recording the aftermath of such miracles; perhaps the poor little creatures are camera shy. Nowadays it only pisces down in remote India or Afghanistan, notably in areas where famine is a constant companion.

Naturally enough, there have been attempts to

update the myth with pseudo-scientific explanations. The favourite story is that giant spouts are responsible – these supposedly pass over lakes and ponds, sucking up all the frogs and fish who then fall to earth when the water spout collapses. Nice idea, but why is the water spout so selective? Why hoover up just the pond life? What happens to all the old wellies, tin cans and algae? Anyway, giant water spouts only occur at sea and are composed primarily of rain water. There is a little sea-water caught up at the base, but nothing to talk about. They are, if you like, rainwater tornadoes, and are therefore devoid of any animal life. Besides, even if a water spout did move inland, no town could have a 300 feet stack of water collapse upon it and then mistake the incident for a rainstorm.

Quite why otherwise sane people are willing to believe such utter rubbish is itself a mystery. It just goes to prove that if you say something often enough, loud enough, people will accept it as the truth.

■ ■ ■

Not only pop and film stars adopt false names: there have been plenty of politicos who have followed suit for one reason or another. Stalin, for example, means man of steel, his real name being Dzhugashvili. Another Russian, born Vyacheslav Skriabin, preferred to be known as Molotov, meaning The Hammer, but he had nothing to do with the petrol bomb so named. It was the Finns who first used these against their Russian invaders in 1939. They calling them Molotov cocktails as a dig at Molotov who was then the Russian Minister of Foreign Affairs.

In the Germany of 1933 a young man named Herbert Karl Frahm found himself on a Gestapo death list for attempting to organise a general strike. He escaped to Norway using forged papers and joined the resistance. After the war he returned to his native Germany as the Norwegian press attaché but became involved in domestic politics, still using the name of those forged papers – Willy Brandt.

David Green of Plonsk in Poland decided he might do better in Israeli politics if he called himself David Ben-Gurion which does have a nice scriptural ring to it. When the woman born Golda Mabovitz entered the same arena, Ben-Gurion advised her to follow suit, which she did as Golda Meir.

Aspiring black politico Kazumu Banda had been so named due to his mother having visited a witch doctor hoping for a cure for her apparent infertility. She received a preparation of root herbs and conceived shortly after, resulting in her calling the happy arrival Kazumu since, in her language, it meant a little root. When later wishing to be taken seriously by the West, Little Root assumed the name Hastings from a local missionary called John Hastings who happened to be a close friend.

Now you might be thinking that all this name changing is a little daft – after all, what's in a name? But it really does matter. Take this example: grand opera written by an Italian Master named Giuseppe Verdi has quite a charismatic tone, hasn't it? Now ask yourself if *The Strumpet* by Joe Green carries the aesthetic impact as *La Traviata* by Giuseppe Verdi. It loses something in the translation, doesn't it?

■ ■ ■

If there is one expression that sums up the concept of maintaining a fashionable style, it is 'keeping up with the Joneses'. And one way of keeping up with the Joneses is to roar round in, for example a Ferrari. However that name is nothing more than the Italian equivalent of 'Smith', words like 'ferrous' being directly linked with it. But someone announcing that he trundles from traffic-jam to traffic-jam in a four and a half pint Smith does not conjure up the same image as someone beating the traffic in a 2.5 litre Ferrari. And, of course, image is what the style game is all about.

Back to the expression in hand. In 1913, a cartoon called 'Keeping up with the Joneses' began a long and successful run in the *New York Globe*. It dealt with the problems that faced those who felt the need to maintain a 'front'. Penned by Arthur Momand, the strip was originally planned as 'Keeping up with the Smiths'. However, as his neighbours were actually called Smith and the idea had evolved from some of the manoeuvres that he went through with them, he decided against that title and went for the next common name that came to mind.

Talking about Smiths, why do we consider horse-shoes to be lucky? There are quite a few ideas tied up in this belief, not least of which is that fact that a horseshoe on its side represents the letter 'C' as in the first letter of the name of Christ. Fire and iron were both once held to be sacred and these two elements came together in the manufacture of horseshoes.

Their 'magic' was proved in the uneducated minds of our forefathers because they could be fitted almost red-hot to a horse's hoof without the animal feeling any pain.

Last but not least comes the legend that Satan approached St Dunstan, who was renowned for his skill as a farrier, requesting to be re-shod. Pretending to fail to see through Satan's disguise, the saint agreed to the task but then tied the Devil down and tortured him until he promised never again to enter premises with a horseshoe on display.

▪ ▪ ▪

American politics have always been the undignified, gaudy, circus-type affairs that they are today, which is why we have the expression 'to jump on the bandwagon'. In the days before the dubious bounties of television and mass media, the first thing that a candidate would do upon arriving at a town was to hire a wagon large enough to accommodate himself, his entourage and a small band, whose job it was to play through the streets and attract attention. Let's face it, everyone loves a parade.

Any local figure who felt so inclined could climb on to the wagon as it moved through the town, thus indicating to the locals their support for the candidate. This could go a long way to securing votes, a favour which was expected to be returned should the man attain office. Since most of the lesser local figures would wait for a lead from the more prominent ones, the expression took on its unsavoury overtones.

If there are two things for which American administrations and police forces are internationally renowned, they are inefficiency and corruption, or as our colonial cousins prefer, 'graft'.

In Ireland, the North of England and certain parts of Scotland, 'grafter' was once an everyday name for the type of flat, rectangular spade ideal for trenching and grave-digging. Indeed, 'graft' is simply a variant of 'grave'. The tool really came into its own when used for squaring off the ditch and 'skimming' the bottom flat, this second purpose giving rise to the Americanism after immigrants had taken the tool and the name with them to their new lives in the States. 'Graft' first put on its shady overcoat in New York during the prohibition era. At that time the Irish virtually manned the entire police department, which was so bent that it rightly earned the reputation for being the best police force money could buy. Talk about two countries divided by a common language, America uses 'graft' to describe skimming off profits or dipping into the municipal till and we employ the word to denote sheer hard work as indeed ditch-digging is if you have ever tried it.

Two common misconceptions about American English are that 'fender' means 'bumper' and that 'fall' is a modern term for autumn. To the Americans, 'fender' actually means that part of a car that we call the wing, and 'fall' is really an extremely old English word that can be found in the writings of Dryden and Shakespeare.

■ ■ ■

It turned out to be a black day for the Nazis when Jessie Owens turned up at the Berlin Olympics in 1936 to run rings around the best that the Fatherland could muster. It has been widely asserted that Owens never received any medals but he did, five of them just to prove his point – Hitler simply refused to present them or congratulate Owens on his victories.

Nor could Owens out-run top-class race horses – he only had a publicity stunt that made it appear as if he could. Owens always made sure that the horse was a thoroughbred. Not only did this look good, but it ensured a high-spirited and skittish animal. The starter then made sure that the starting pistol went off right in the horse's ear, causing it to throw one almighty wobbler and rear and plunge all over the place. Also, man accelerates to his top speed in a fraction of the time it takes a horse to get into top gear. So, this trick with the pistol ensured that by the time the jockey had got his mount running, Owens was halfway down the track. For the latter part of the race, the horse gained rapidly on Owens, covering over three yards for every one of his. But it was too late for the animal to win because Owens always insisted on a hundred-yard race. By Owens' own admission, if he had to compete over 110 yards he would have lost every time.

Talking about the Berlin Olympics, did you know that was the first time the ceremony of the Olympic flame was performed? It may seem to be a symbol of great antiquity but it was Hitler who came up with the idea and organised an impressive series of athletes to relay the torch all the way from Greece to Berlin. Maybe he got the idea from burning down the Reichstag.

When declaring open the Hollywood-style Los Angeles games President Reagan fell into the trap of stating the 'twenty-third Olympiad open'. This would be pretty difficult since 'Olympiad' properly describes the gap of four years between each meeting and thus cannot commence until the cessation of the games.

■ ■ ■

Industrial action has not always been taken by a workforce demanding higher wages. There have been several instances when workers have demanded a pay reduction in order to safeguard their jobs.

In 1884 the powerful Sockmakers Union of Leicestershire threatened a walk-out if the employers refused to reduce pay by seven and a half per cent. The workers had decided this was the necessary step to make the industry more competitive and thereby secure more work.

In 1843, 8,000 Durham and Northumberland miners went on strike when the management turned down a petition demanding that all men should be restricted to three shillings a day to reduce over-heads and secure the future of the pits.

As recently as 1937, all the brickmakers of Jordonow near Cracow in Poland voted to hold a sit-in for lower pay which they saw as the only way to produce cheaper bricks, gain more export orders and thereby reduce unemployment. How things change!

■ ■ ■

Evanston, Illinois is bang in the middle of America's Bible Belt and in the last century religious fundamentalists in that area held a tight control on things in general. Frivolity on a Sunday was very much off the menu and among the numerous restrictions in the Sunday trading laws was the ban on the sale of ice-cream sodas. But people still had a healthy thirst and after church they headed for the soda-fountains anyway. The thick syrups normally used to flavour the sodas were added neat to the ice creams and knocked out at the same price. Just to rub salt in the wounds of the outraged righteous, the Heath Robinson dish was called an ice-cream Sundae.

Ten-pin bowling was born of similar circumstances after eighteenth-century Puritans succeeded in banning the game of nine-pins as the work of the Devil. Those interested in a bit of devilment simply added another pin and carried on as normal.

■ ■ ■

Whether they deserve it or not, the Scots are saddled with the reputation of being a nation not given to expensive gesture. But the expression 'scot free' has no connection with a reluctant highlander who always has extreme difficulty in locating his pocket every time it is his round.

Skot was merely the Old Norse for a tax or payment and those who attempted to live 'scot free' would nowadays be called tax dodgers. On the other hand, the same reputation did produce the trade name of Scotch Tape.

With the advent of two-tone cars in the 1920s, 3M produced a two-inch wide masking tape for use in the spray shops. In an attempt to minimise the production costs, 3M only applied adhesive along a quarter inch strip down each side of the tape. Because of this cheese-paring the tape kept falling off the cars, but the nickname 'Scotch tape' given it by the motor trade has stuck.

■ ■ ■

The extensive and protracted misuse of the word 'cyclone' to describe whirlwinds of one type or another has robbed the term of its true meaning – there is even a jet engine so named through this misconception. Unfortunately the word does not describe a wind of any sort.

A cyclone is a broad pattern of weather rotating about a centre of low barometric pressure. Influenced by the Coriolis Effect, which is produced by the Earth's rotation, these revolve anti-clockwise in the northern hemisphere and clockwise in the southern.

■ ■ ■

Speaking in Birmingham in 1968 Enoch Powell warned of great disharmony in the country caused by un-checked immigration. What he actually said was: 'As I look ahead I am filled with foreboding. Like the Roman, I seem to see the River Tiber foaming with much blood.' Powell's classical education was to be his undoing.

In ancient Rome the dream of such a phenomenon was a standard portent of impending doom, but no one realised that his infamous words were in quotation marks or even bothered to quote him correctly.

He later stated that the only thing he would have changed in his speech was to utter the quote in Latin to highlight the fact that he was waxing lyrical, not speaking literally.

Ah well, 'a little learning' and all that!

■ ■ ■

Early cities were oases of civilisation amidst a desert of ignorance and superstition where one's country cousin rolled his eyes and leapt out of his goat-skin every time something went bump in the night. The resultant prejudice caused townies to coin 'heathen' which simply meant 'hearth-dweller'. The term shifted to its present meaning as a result of the dark goings-on in rural areas.

Although 'pagan' is a parallel term in that it derives from the Latin *paganus*, a rustic, its history is slightly more complicated. The Romans were a warrior-elite society and a soldier had little time for civvies whom he dismissed, with no religious overtones at all, as 'pagans'. Early Christians called themselves Milites Christi – Soldiers of Christ – and simply applied the Roman soldiers' slur to their persecutors.

■ ■ ■

Back in the good old days when God was for sale and the Church had a stranglehold monopoly on the product, forgiveness was without doubt the best-selling line. On special offer to robber barons and the like was a package deal to heaven designed for those who by rights should have been heading straight for the place where you can't get near the fire for bishops.

What you got for your money was a novena, which was nine days of prayer muttered on your behalf by the vendors. Working on the self-evident principle that you can't take it with you when you go anyway, these were very popular indeed. The prayer-peddlars had a pretty tight schedule in times of plague and crusade.

Their sincerity was a trifle suspect in the eyes of the ordinary person since it seemed that as soon as one prayer-run was over, the monks immediately forgot about it and got stuck into another. This dubious practice gave us the expression 'nine-day wonder'.

■ ■ ■

Although the fighting between Britain and Germany physically came to an end in 1945, the war did not officially end until 1956, and one of the biggest post-war gaffes of the British Government was to reject the Volkswagen factory as part of the German reparations package. Working on the advice of British car manufacturers who said: 'There is no future for an air-cooled, rear-mounted engine car', the British Government rejected the VW factory and, to compound the error magnanimously placed an order for 2,000 cars to help put the plant back on its feet.

Nor is the Mercedes so named after a racy *señorita*

but after the ten-year-old daughter of an Austrian entrepreneur named Emil Jellinek. In 1889 Jellinek entered a Daimler in the Tour de Nice under the pseudonym Herr Mercedes, to honour his daughter. Having won the race, Jellinek negotiated with Daimler for the sole marketing rights in Austria. He continued to use the name Mercedes for his cars and it became so popular that Daimler-Benz had no option but to adopt it.

■ ■ ■

The primitive custom of portraying important figures with an all-over glow, or what we commonly call a halo, has its roots deep in pagan culture and was merely adopted by the Christian church. Just about all Christian tradition is of pagan origin and, off hand, I can't think of a single custom original to the church.

Be that as it may, the luminous glow adorning saints' heads is not a halo, it is a nimbus. Ultimately deriving from the Greek term for a threshing floor, most likely because of the circular path trod by the oxen employed in the operation, 'halo' was first applied to the disc of the sun, the moon, or a shield. It still applies to the luminous glow to be seen about either of those celestial bodies but never to saintly ones.

■ ■ ■

The geometric theorem that the square of the hypotenuse of a triangle equals the sum of the squares on the other two sides is named after Pythagorus but was well known and in application hundreds of years before the man was supposedly born in 581BC. If indeed he was born at all – not everyone accepts he ever existed. He was perhaps a little like Homer or Aesop, a composite figure embracing a collection of theories or philosophies.

The theorem was widely used by the Egyptians who, after all, were the kings of the pyramid world. It was also used by the Babylonians before that. It is true that nobody went around making a big fuss about the theorem, stating it to be a new-found truth and so forth. To those numerous people who were aware of the fact, it would have been stating the obvious.

■ ■ ■

People love to hold ozone responsible for the allegedly bracing effect of sea air. As usual though, the reality is somewhat less romantic; that tang is the odour of rotting seaweed and a variety of decomposing marine life. That is just as well, too, since ozone in concentrations above a mere few parts per million is actually fatal to man. Ozone lies in the upper atmosphere, where it blocks out harmful ultra-violet light and radiation. It contains three oxygen atoms – one of which is highly reactive – and would rapidly act on the lungs in much the same way as ordinary air rusts metal. Since ozone is super-rich in oxygen, it is ironic that people exposed to the gas would actually suffocate after it had attacked their lungs.

■ ■ ■

A real mother-lovin', all-American boy was Colonel Paul W. Tibbets Jnr. So much so that he even named his B29 bomber 'Enola Gay' in her honour and, to carve her name with pride in the history books, he took off in it bound for Hiroshima on 6 August 1945.

Post-war groups, opposing this new, nuclear horror eventually gathered under a symbol with an interesting origin. The Ban the Bomb motif, as seen on all good 2CVs, is based on semaphore. In this, the letter 'N' is given by the signaller holding both flags out at forty-five degrees to each side, pointing down at the ground, and the letter 'D' is indicated by his holding one flag high above the head with the other pointing at the feet. Superimpose one on top of the other and there you are.

■ ■ ■

The superstition admonishing all to avoid passing beneath ladders has two parents – not the least of which is the fact that any triangle was once held sacred in that it was perceived symbolic of the Holy Trinity and so to break it automatically invited ill-fortune.

The other influence is far more worldly and tangible since a ladder propped up against the wall was once a favourite impromptu gallows with the rope dangling from the top rung. The superstitious felt that to place themselves in such an area might well presage a suspended sentence.

Few had a more complex system of beliefs and taboos than the Ancient Egyptians who were convinced that their goddess Bast assumed the guise of a black cat to mingle with her faithful either at the temple or *en route* to worship and, needless to say, good luck and great fortune would be bestowed upon all those whose paths she crossed. Indeed to kill any cat in Egypt, even if by accident, resulted in stoning to death on the spot.

Anyway, Roman soldiers on active service in Egypt or elsewhere in North Africa picked up the belief in the form of a semi-seriously held superstition and then brought it with them on their tour of the British Isles. The strong association between the black cat and Egypt – land of the Black Arts – went more than a long way to securing for the black cat the position of witches' familiar.

Our forefathers were heavily into the worship of trees which they regarded as the dwelling places of a variety of deities and spirits. If help was required in some venture or other the person concerned would toddle off to the forest and lay hands on the appropriate type of tree for the god required and then make their request. Today this little ritual survives in the expression 'touch wood' which, in America, is more frequently heard as 'knock-on wood'.

Although shaking hands is today almost universally recognised as a gesture of friendly intent this custom would appear to have been born out of distrust and fear. When, for example, the leaders of armies wished to have a quick pow-wow prior to the kick-off of some blood-bath or other they would stand in the no man's land between the two hosts gripping each other's right wrist to prevent either sneakily drawing sword and spoiling any chance of a good battle. Each army watched keenly this grip and should either general relinquish his grasp both sides waded in. Gradually this practice reduced to the familiar gesture of a handshake which was then taken to be a solemn indication of lack of intent to draw arms.

▪ ■ ▪

The friendly little gesture much favoured by British road users and made famous by Harvey Smith is indeed one of great antiquity.

With monotonous regularity there are printed tales claiming the V sign to have been born after various engagements throughout the Hundred Years War but these are all nonsense. Irrespective of which battle is nominated the story goes that the French, understandably miffed at constantly getting the pointed end of the stick from English archers, lost what little sang-froid they had left and issued a dire threat. Prior to the set-to the French sent word that not only were they going to give the English a right royal stuffing but that after the battle they would amputate the relevant two fingers from any surviving archers' right hands to prevent them ever drawing bow again.

The French vaunting was to no avail as the English kebabed them yet again and, just to add insult to injury, the archers lined up after the blood-bath and waved the two relevant fingers at what was left of the French army.

It is such a lovely story that it's almost a sacrilege

to shoot holes in it, but the sign was known long before any such sport with the French – indeed long before the introduction of the long bow itself which, incidentally, is drawn with three fingers and not two. Besides, it's far more likely that any English archer unfortunate enough to fall into French hands would have lost far more intimate bits and pieces to impromptu surgery.

The sign has long associations with the occult, being used to ward off the devil when used in a downward sweep, intending to block his horns and prevent him rising up to inflict mischief on the user. Should one of our ancestors have felt sufficiently ill-disposed to one of his neighbours as to wish the devil upon him he would then have used the sign in the conventional manner. This, it was believed, would result in the devil rearing up to inflict black fortune on the recipient.

The gesture did not acquire sexual connotations or overtones until late medieval times when the V sign merged with yet another two fingered gesture as made by the index and little finger being extended from the clenched fist. Still greatly favoured by our continental cousins this gesture was, and still is, intended to represent the horns of the cuckold which in olden days was taken as a pretty hefty insult. Gradually the now traditional V took over, probably because it's an easier gesture to make and so much more venom can be injected into the violent upswing of the hand.

The gesture is still used in magic circles and prior to the Second World War many of England's white witches assembled on the White Cliffs of Dover and held a ceremony culminating in the massed brandishing of Harvey Smiths across the channel, the intention being to bring the Devil and downfall to A. Hitler & Co. Presumably the cynical would say that this was highly ineffective whilst adherents to the magical arts can claim that, in the long run, the trick worked.

■ ■ ■

Even in this country it is the custom – albeit a mite tongue in cheek – to employ the cry of 'Geronimo!' just prior to mock heroics. The sarcasm implied is there because we picked up the shout from the Americans, who used it quite seriously, when they were considered to be 'over-paid, over-sexed and over here'.

The whole thing began back in the formative days of the United States 82nd Airborne Division, which trained at Lafayette in Indiana. In 1938, recruits were given leave on the day before their first full-drill jump from a plane. Most drifted into town and a fair number went to the cinema showing a film entitled *Geronimo*. The film included a stunt based on a real incident in the eponymous Indian's life, when he rode off a vertical cliff in Oklahoma, named Medicine Bluffs, to escape his Army pursuers who, quite sensibly, decided not to follow suit. In the film, the stuntman yelled 'Geronimo!' as he plummeted into the river. The incident caused much sniggering and nervous shifting about in their seats in an audience who knew that they themselves had a date with gravity the next morning.

Before hurling themselves bodily into space with nothing between themselves and extinction but a fine silk mushroom, many mimicked the stuntman in what was most likely a nervous attempt to cover up their own fear. And that was that! The next thing that anyone knew, all the recruits were yelling 'Geronimo!' and the 82nd had little choice but to adopt it formally as a battle cry.

As for the name of the Indian himself this too has a tale to tell. The superb *guerrillero* (this is the proper term for a fighter – *guerrilla* is the Spanish for 'little war' and *guerrillero* is the term for the fighter who employs such tactics) was born Goyathlay, meaning 'he who yawns'. After his family were slaughtered by the Mexicans he repeatedly harried them with night attacks causing them to bestow the nickname of Geronimo. In Spanish there is a popular expression *Sine un Hieronimo de douda* which is understood to mean 'without a shadow of a doubt'. Quite how (St) Jerome's name fell to such use is obscure but since Goyathlay struck like a shadow in the night the Mexicans called him Geronimo.

■ ■ ■

Two of the most famous assassinations ever are those of Presidents Lincoln and Kennedy and, even though I am not one for the supernatural, the following is enough to raise the most sceptical of eyebrows.

Lincoln first entered Congress in 1846, Kennedy followed in 1946. Lincoln became president in November 1860, and Kennedy followed in November 1960.

Both were succeeded by southern senators named Johnson: Andrew Johnson being born in 1808, L. B. Johnson in 1908.

Booth, Lincoln's killer, was born in 1839 and Oswald, Kennedy's alleged killer, in 1939. Both killers were

Southerners, and were shot before coming to trial, most likely to shut them up.

Booth fired in a theatre and escaped via a warehouse; Oswald fired from a warehouse and ran into a theatre.

A matter of hours before their deaths, both presidents are recorded as making strikingly similar and sadly prophetic statements.

To W. H. Crook, one of his bodyguards, Lincoln said that he felt sure that he would soon be a target for assassination. 'And I have no doubt that they will succeed. If it is to be done, it is impossible to prevent it.'

Kennedy, to his personal adviser Ken O'Donnell, said: 'If anybody wants to shoot the President of the United States, it's not a very hard job. All you need is a high building and a telescopic rifle, and there's nothing anyone can do to prevent it.' That proved to be the day.

Both presidents were vigorous civil rights campaigners and both were shot in the back of the head on a Friday while in the company of their wives. Lincoln was shot in Ford's Theatre, Kennedy in a Ford Lincoln car. Both had been advised by their secretaries to alter their engagements on the fatal days and reduce public appearances for a while.

Kennedy's secretary was called Lincoln and, you've guessed it, Lincoln's secretary was called Kennedy.

It makes you think a bit, doesn't it?

■ ■ ■

Warfare

When it comes to man's favourite hobby of warfare, he demonstrates uncharacteristic selflessness by permitting other species to join in the fun and be slaughtered too. And have there been some weird conscripts.

In the Second World War, the Russians trained dogs to associate the underneath of tanks with food. When confronted with advancing panzers, they released packs of half-starved dogs with mines strapped to their backs. But the dogs had been better trained than anyone imagined and they identified as food sources only the tanks with which they had been trained, so they happily and hungrily chased Russian tanks all over the place.

Towards the end of the same conflict, hundreds of American soldiers rounded up millions of bats – to pilot the 'bat bomb'. Hours before the first full test, thousands of the bats escaped and destroyed a large area of the training base. The scheme was abandoned.

When the US Navy trained dolphins to act as kamikaze torpedoes the animals performed perfectly during tests but for some reason many refused to carry the real explosive packs.

■ ■ ■

The bikini has its etymological roots in something far more sinister than scantily-pantied maidens frolicking on sun-kissed beaches for it takes its name from Bikini Atoll in the Marshall Islands which, in 1946, was chosen by the United States as an atomic test site. Despite their protestations that they were quite unworthy of the honour, the inhabitants of the island were nevertheless evicted so their betters could spend the next twelve years popping off atomic devices to see what would happen to the place.

In the same year as the first test a French car engineer named Louis Reard joined his mother's clothing company and in response to a call for something new and revolutionary, Louis came up with a two piece swim-suit. He stated he named his brain-child the bikini as an analogy between the effect of a beautiful woman so clad and the bombs dropped on the island. No doubt's Bikini's wild life just died laughing at Reard's little jest.

■ ■ ■

Many assume the sinking of the *Lusitania* to be an action resulting in America's involvement in the First World War, but it achieved no such end. America made all the right noises; Theodore Roosevelt quivered in righteous indignation as he screamed 'Piracy' and all that guff but then he just sat back and let the matter slide. The *Lusitania* was torpedoed on 7 May 1915 which was a good two years before America joined in the fun and, at the end of the day, out of the death toll of 1,198 only 120 were Americans.

As for the ship having been an innocent passenger liner sunk without warning by the filthy Hun, this too is a long way from the truth. The Germans had issued countless warnings – both verbal and written – which should have left Britain and every one of her ships' captains in absolutely no doubt what the Germans intended to do to British shipping. They had mounted a blockade of the British Isles and were getting more than a little fed up of refraining from taking pot-shots at 'innocent' passenger ships. On the very day the *Lusitania* sailed from New York the German government took space on the front page of the *New York World* to reiterate all these warnings. In that notice – which they rather pointedly placed slap-bang next-door to Cunard's announcement of the imminent departure of the *Lusitania*, the Germans gave clear warning that any ship attempting to run the blockade would find itself the target of submarine attack. The message could only have been clearer had they written it on a bit of four-by-two and beat the *Lusitania*'s captain over the head with it.

The Cunard executive took the warnings seriously enough and cabled the captain to assume a zigzag course on the way home and steer clear of all land-falls, but for reasons best known to the captain himself, both these instructions were ignored. The *Lusitania* was holding a steady course at the reduced speed of twenty-one knots as she passed near the land-fall of the Old Head of Kinsale in Southern Ireland. In this manner the *Lusitania* presented herself as a sitting target to the captain of the U-20 who scored two direct hits causing the boilers to blow and the *Lusitania* to sink like a stone.

As for her being an 'innocent passenger liner' she was carrying a goodly number of Canadian volunteer troops, 5,000 cases of munitions and a consignment of fulminate of mercury fuses – and that's what the British were prepared to own up to. All said and done we had been at war with Germany for over ten months at the time so it is rather difficult to see what all the righteous indignation was about. If my memory serves me well, the British government was getting its knickers in a twist over some chappie in the Gulf using 'human shields', but I suppose that's different.

At the end of the day it comes down to who wins the war and who gets to write the history books. Everybody has heard of the vile and cowardly sinking of the *Lusitania* but no one seems to have got into a similar tiswas over the 1945 sinking of the unarmed German liner *Wilhelm Gustloff*, which went down taking 8,000 women and children with her.

■ ■ ■

The superstition regarding the taking of the third light for a cigarette arose from a justifiable fear experienced by British troops in the Boer War. The third light was indeed unlucky since the rule of thumb dictated that an enemy sniper's attention would be attracted at night by the lighting of the match; in the time it took to pass the match to the second man the sniper would have his rifle into position and lined up so the third man wouldn't even get a chance to read the health warning!

■ ▪ ■

In the First World War the brain-children of Sir Ernest Swinton were moved up to the front where their debut caused large numbers of the Kaiser's finest to be suddenly possessed of an overwhelming desire to transfer to the Navy. Now appearing laughably cumbersome on old news-reel footage these first tanks had nevertheless a colossal psychological impact on the enemy.

The covert operation to move these leviathans to the front had one major headache – how the bloody hell do you move something that size and keep it secret? Sir Ernest came up with the idea of shipping them by rail encased in massive wooden crates, each sporting the legend BULK WATER CARRIERS. This earned them the nickname 'tank' which stuck for good.

■ ▪ ■

'Jeep' is one of the rare cases in the field of word origins where fact is stranger than fiction, in that the designation 'GP' had nothing to do with the origin of the term.

The first version of the vehicle were produced by the Bantam Car Company and attracted the nickname 'jeep' long before the Ford-manufactured GPV came into existence. In 1936 E. C. Segar introduced a new character, Eugene the Jeep, into his ever-popular Popeye cartoon. A tough little dog-like creature who could only say 'jeep, jeep', Eugene could go anywhere, do anything and could become invisible at will. Since the GIs thought there were many parallel character-istics, except that one ran on orchids and the other on petrol, the name 'jeep' was promptly bestowed on the vehicle.

■   ■   ■

It is unclear whether 'Viking' is derived from the Old Norse *vik*, meaning a bay or creek, or from some term associated with *wick*, as meaning village or specific vicinity. Either way, the proper pronunciation of the term should make it rhyme with 'picking' and not 'spiking'.

Be they the men of the fjords or the men of the vil-lages, the Vikings popped over here with monotonous regularity to duff up the locals. In emulation of their warrior god, Vikings would attack either clad in bearskins or stark naked, howling and chewing on their sword blades the while, which certainly had the desired effect of scaring our forefathers out of their goatskins. Either from *bjorn serkr*, bear-shirt, or *berr serkr*, bare of shirt, the Vikings gave their savage warrior god the name Berserk. The lamentable displays of undignified frenzy undertaken by his emu-lators left the deity's name in English to stand for any irrational outburst.

Some time around the ninth century Viking raiders into Ireland imposed what came to be known as the Nose Tax, so called for those who failed to pay had their noses slit open. This appears to be the source of the otherwise inexplicable expression 'paying through the nose'.

■ ■ ■

In the days of old when knights were bold and so forth, should two aspiring dragon-slayers meet when out riding and both keep visor firmly down, then it was odds on that battle would commence. Should one or both wish to indicate friendship, then visors would be lifted and the hand movement involved in this gesture survives as the modern military salute which conveys if not friendship then at least respect.

Should a knight be romantically involved with a lady of the court she would often indicate her favour for this knight by handing him some item of her clothing – usually a scarf – which he would then tie about his right elbow when taking to the jousting field to compete as her champion. Since every one could see just who had tapped off with whom this gave rise to the expression 'wearing your heart on your sleeve'.

The war-lance of old was pretty heavy and difficult to control if held horizontal whilst the horse blundered across uneven ground. For as long as possible the lance was held vertical and then, in an action called tilting, it was gradually lowered to come to bear on the target as range closed. By the time the lance had been fully lowered the knight had also reached full speed which is why 'full tilt' came to mean just that.

On the subject of armour it is worth dismissing

that greatest of all myths – this being that the weight of a full suit was so excessive that knights needed winching a-horse by crane.

The average suit of armour weighed no more than sixty pounds and the heaviest suit ever made was produced in 1570 by the Royal Workshop at Greenwich for the third Earl of Worcester. That suit weighed just over eighty-one pounds which is several pounds lighter than the full marching kit of a Second World War British infantryman. A knight was an extremely important piece of medieval armament which was expected to remain on the field all day, something he would be unable to do if strapped down by several hundred pounds worth of iron.

■　■　■

Hitler's name was Hitler, it was not Schicklegrüber. Hitler was the son of Alois Hitler, a shoemaker turned customs officer, and his third wife Karla Poelzl, a girl twenty-three years his junior who had been a maid in his first wife's house. Alois had been born out of wedlock to Maria Anna Schicklegrüber and Johann Huettler, that couple not marrying until their son was five. Alois did not legally hold his father's name, variously spelt Heuttler, Hitler and Hiedler, until he was thirty-five. By the time young Adolph appeared the family name was definitely and legally Hitler. The 'Schicklegrüber' tag was revived by his political opponents in the 1930s and eagerly seized on by the Allied propaganda machine to ridicule him.

Hitler never worked as a house-painter but, like Churchill, was not a bad hand with brush and canvas.

In fact, there are some who say that had he persisted he probably would have been accepted by the Berlin Academy and we could have missed out on the Second World War.

Without doubt, the best loved of all the Hitler myths is that he ended up absolutely gaga with syphilis. That the man was mad as a hatter is probably beyond dispute, but it doesn't seem that he was clinically insane. Heavily into astrology and other sorts of hokum it was perhaps inevitable that Hitler should appoint a quack to be his personal physician; it was sheer coincidence that Theo Morell was also Berlin's most fashionable pox-doctor.

As the fall of Berlin became inevitable Morell high-tailed it to the Allied lines taking with him Hitler's medical records, these documents providing more than one or two surprises. The old joke about his mono-testicular state transpired to be absolutely true, but this condition is not exactly rare. Most incredible of all is the regular medication which Morell cheerfully acknowledged to have been prescribing for Hitler.

Supposedly a miracle cure for Hitler's dyspepsia, Morell was feeding the little corporal capsules containing the live bacteria from Bulgarian peasants' stools; quite why the peasants had to be Bulgarian was never explained. Anything up to three times a day, Morell was injecting der Reichs-bottom with a mixture of vitamins and amphetamines which made Hitler feel on top of the wold he wanted to dominate. This excessive use of amphetamines explains a lot of things, such as his highly agitated states in which he summoned his generals at four in the morning to harangue them for hours on end. So, not only was Hitler unbalanced at both ends, it is grotesquely amusing that the German war effort was being orchestrated by a vicious little corporal who was strung out on speed and, quite literally, full of you know what.

■   ■   ■

Properly 'random' means of or pertaining to the outer limit of operation, and in early artillery parlance a gun firing at random was on maximum elevation and sacrificing accuracy in the quest for range. Since the shots fell where they may the term crept towards its current meaning.

Conversely, if a piece of ordinance was so close to the target as to be able to be fired without any elevation whatsoever it was said to be fixed 'point blank'. This is a corruption of the French *point blanc*, the white inner of a target, and the term came to mean what it does today through the cannon being pointed straight at the objective like a pistol levelled at a target.

Towards the end of the First World War the Germans produced a massive gun with which they shelled Paris from a distance of seventy-odd miles. Although the gun was in fact made by Skoda, the allied press mistakenly thought it had been made in one of the munitions factories run by Frau Bertha Krupp. Thus the gun was christened 'Big Bertha', a term surviving still as an epithet for a woman of more than generous proportions.

During the Second World War the Germans made much use of a multi-barrelled mortar, the shells from which emitted a highly distinctive moaning sound.

In German, the piece of equipment was known as *Minenwerfer*, literally a mine-thrower, which caused Allied troops to christen it Moaning Minnie which later shifted into civvy street to describe an habitual whinge.

■ ■ ■

Although 'garnish' is now rarely heard outside the kitchen it started life in the jargon of medieval warmongers. Originally the word meant 'to warn', but in particular to alert a town of impending attack. This having been done, the battlements would be arrayed with all the paraphernalia of medieval defence and the fortifications then stood garnished. Nearly all early platter decorations were representations of knights and machines of war and when these gave way to various bits of greenery and fancy-cut vegetables the term remained unchanged.

The unwary schemer who is caught out by his own plans and 'hoist on his own petard' recalls one of the earliest explosive devices used for breaching castle gates or walls. These petards were notoriously unreliable and would quite often capriciously explode as soon as the unfortunate sapper put a match anywhere near them, he then being blown in the air, or hoist, by his own device. One can only assume that the petard made an extremely unusual noise upon detonation since it took its name from the French *petarde*, a succession of farts as emitted by a horse. The partridge of pear tree fame is named from the same source due to the pronounced whirring of its wings on take off.

The notion that 'zap' is a 1930s American comicism is quashed by the following quote from 1660 and listed in the OED under Zappe: 'When that rampart which is, shall either be beaten or zapped'. Ultimately derived from the Italian *zappare*, to inflict damage with explosives, people have been talking about zapping things for years – the original zapper is now known in English as a sapper. The use of 'zap' has long been colloquial in Italian – especially amongst the Mafia who used it to mean kill – and doubtless the influence of that nation and organisation in America caused the term to shift into general parlance.

■ ■ ■

Those given to bouts of histrionics are described as 'going over the top', an expression which started life in the trenches of the First World War. Prior to an infantry attack the enemy emplacements would be softened up with artillery fire, the accuracy of which was corrected by spotters in captive balloons. When the troops in the trenches saw these balloons winched up into the sky they knew trouble lay ahead for them, hence 'the balloon goes up'. Not long after this some officer blew a whistle and the infantry were expected to charge out 'over the top' of the trench and charge manfully into enemy machine-gun fire. The attendant shouting, screaming and general leaping about that this entailed engendered the modern usage.

The first wave of infantry attack was the original 'forlorn hope', an expression ultimately rooted in the Dutch *verloren hoop*, meaning a lost troop. Otherwise known in French as *les enfants perdus*, it was doubtless the fact that such troops looked forlorn and didn't have a hope in hell of survival which caused the spelling change.

■ ■ ■

When the army of old went on the move the restricted communications of the day produced a logistical nightmare. Apart from the fact that available transport was less than efficient the column attracted great numbers of hangers-on, collectively known as camp followers. A goodly number of these tended to be women – some of whom provided legitimate laundry and cleaning services whilst others provided services indicating their total misunderstanding of the old maxim, 'An army marches on its stomach'. Since these women tramped along at the rear of the column with the baggage train it was not long before 'old bag' or 'baggage' moved into general usage to denote a woman to whom nature had been less than kind.

Because of the thieving nature of most camp followers, an officer's aide always travelled at the rear of the column to protect personal possessions from those of the light fingers. The pack saddles were known as 'bats', hence 'batman'. In French such saddles were known as a *bast*, and were so constructed as to convert to a makeshift bed for a night on the trail. Given the premise that a child conceived on a mule driver's bast was unlikely to be the product of a sanctified union, it is not too 'ard' to guess what word this produced.

Always moving ahead of the column to organise food and billeting was an officer designated the Harbinger, this being derived from two terms in Old

German – *heri*, and *berga*, these meaning 'army' and 'shelter' respectively. When a harbinger turned up in a village or town it always boded ill for the locals who knew they were going to have a bunch of squaddies foisted on them producing a lot of aggro and no return – the only people ever pleased to see a harbinger were the local innkeepers and the anthology of pros. The resentment with which the main body of the population regarded the arrival of a harbinger relegated his title to mean a portent of imminent disaster.

■ ■ ■

If the Gauls hadn't attacked Rome and laid siege to The Citadel then money would have been called Lord knows what.

In a spectacular action the Gauls had actually taken control of vast areas of the city and had dug in for a good fight. Under cover of darkness they attempted a sneak attack at night and were actually scaling the walls of the Citadel undetected by the Roman guard. Some geese sacred to the Temple of Juno became agitated and the centurions turned out in force to give Johnny Barbarian a right good seeing to.

As a reward to the goddess she was thenceforth revered as Juno Moneta, this last term meaning 'she who warns'. Many years later the main temple erected to her under this title was used to house the Roman mint and the resultant coinage took its name from the goddess.

A much misused term today is 'decimate', invariably used to mean wholesale or total slaughter, whereas it means to kill one tenth only. Common as a field punishment in Roman days was the lining up of a legion that had attempted mutiny or shown cowardice in the face of the enemy, whilst officers went along slitting the throats of every tenth man. Had the legion been successful in combat a monument was constructed of captured weapons and placed on the battle field at a point where events turned in Roman favour – and from the Greek *tropos*, a turning, we derive 'trophy'.

It was also common for victorious Roman naval commanders to hack off the prows of vanquished enemy shipping and haul them back to Rome where they were used to decorate the speaker's platform in the Roman Forum. In Latin a ship's prow was called a *rostrum*, this now denoting any orator's platform.

■ ■ ■

Not that there is anything warlike about the Labour Party any more, but it is nevertheless surprising that the Fabian Society takes its name from a Roman general who stood about six goose-steps to the right of Mussolini.

Quintus Fabius Maximus was appointed by the Senate to settle once and for all the problem of Hannibal and his Carthaginian rabble. Instead of tackling his adversary head-on, Fabius opted for snapping tactics – sudden night attacks, enticing Hannibal ever onwards to draw thin his lines of supply and contact, constantly manoeuvring him into hilly terrain where the Carthaginian cavalry was less than useless. Until these tactics were validated Fabius got a lot of earache in Rome where the general feeling was that he should stop pussy-footing about and get stuck in. The Senate even took to calling him Cunctator – The Delayer – but, at the end of the day, when his strategies proved successful Fabius retained the insult not only as a badge of honour but as a thumb-to-the-nose to his detractors.

When the socialist society was formed in the winter of 1883 the members firmly opted to turn their backs on all the hard-line lefties and steer a course away from actual revolution. The group avowed to bring about their desired social changes by a slow process of reasoning and the education of governments and people alike. It was for this option that they took their name from Fabius.

Another cavalry of the ancient world to survive in English phraseology is that of the Parthians. Highly skilled horsemen, their party piece was to feign a disarrayed retreat which invariably prompted their adversaries to pursue them with much enthusiastic whooping and shouting. At this point the Parthians would turn in the saddle and, having perfected the act of firing a bow to the rear at full gallop, would cut their pursuers to smithereens. Originally properly issued as a 'Parthian shot', the insult now hurled over the shoulders on point of departure is called a parting shot, this alteration in spelling being occasioned only by the time of delivery.

■ ■ ■

The high points of most revolutions are invariably more important in their symbolism than in their actual achievements. When the French rabble took the Bastille they fully expected to liberate countless martyrs to their cause but they only effected the release of a couple of forgers, one nobleman and two lunatics. Had the mob struck a few days earlier they would have unleashed the Marquis de Sade to boot. As it turned out the mob did the Administration a favour; the prison had become far too expensive to run and was scheduled for demolition.

Even further into the realms of farce lies the storming of the Winter Palace in Russia. Despite the countless massive, brooding paintings depicting the noble Russian peasantry marching resolutely into the withering gunfire from the Winter Palace to take their place in destiny, the reality was an absolute fiasco. There was no last-ditch shoot out between the Bolsheviks and Kerensky's government on the night of 7 November 1917.

Nothing much was happening on this day so the Bolsheviks decided to send an ultimatum to Kerensky at the palace. A messenger was duly delegated the task but when he got outside he found that someone had stolen his truck leaving him a long walk. He eventually found a bicycle but by the time he arrived at the palace and delivered the message there was only five minutes of the allotted time left to run. Part of the note informed Kerensky that the guns of the cruiser *Aurora* and those of the *Fortress of Peter and Paul*, were trained on the palace and had instructions to give the palace a serious pounding prior to massive infantry attack. This was more than enough for Kerensky who had had a belly-full of politics anyway, so he told the messenger to hurry home with the answer that all conditions were agreeable. This was not the messenger's night; when he got outside the palace he found someone had nicked his bike.

Kerensky assembled the palace's 'defenders' – a small detachment of cadets and a woman's battalion – and told them that the game had been played and that the best thing that they could do was to ditch their uniforms and run around shouting 'Up the Revolution!'. Meanwhile, back at the ranch, the Bolsheviks, unwitting of their messenger's problems assumed the absence of a reply to be a curt refusal to their terms. So, not being a bunch of chaps to back down, they decided to flash the pre-arranged signal to the *Aurora* and let them get on with the business. Trouble was, the pre-arranged signal involved a red lantern and no one could find one. When something was finally cobbled together the lantern was brandished and the *Aurora* and the *Fort* lit up the sky with an awesome barrage . . . of blanks – the only ammunition they had.

Not to be outdone in the dignity stakes the Bolsheviks marched on the palace anyway. There was some sporadic gunfire around the grounds and this resulted in the death of six invaders, all of whom were shot by their comrades in the confusion. Meanwhile, Kerensky, also unaware of the messenger's problems, got fed up of waiting for someone to whom he could surrender and, at a loss for anything more constructive to do, he simply wandered out to his car and drove off. He later recorded his laughing at the irony of the idiot Bolshevik guards on the gate saluting him on his departure. Back at the palace the Bolsheviks were still scampering around looking for him but were hopelessly lost in the labyrinth of the palace's 2,000-odd rooms.

■ ■ ■

One of the most famous quotations of British military history is the Duke of Wellington's alleged observation that, 'The Battle of Waterloo was won on the playing fields of Eton.' Wellington never said anything so stupid.

He had little time for the British public-school ethos and even less time for Eton college itself. He had attended the school for a short time before his parents removed him since they did not consider his academic ability sufficient to warrant the expenditure of funds better spent on his brothers Gerald and Henry who were brighter pupils. Wellington once went as far as making a point of refusing to give sixpence to a collection organised to raise funds to effect improvements at the school.

Like all good apocrypha this 'quotation' did not make an appearance until well after the Duke was safely tucked up in the big battlefield in the sky and unable to scotch it for the rubbish it was. The attribution first appeared in 1855 in a book entitled *The Political Future of England* by Count Charles de Montalembert and takes the form of, 'It is here that the Battle of Waterloo was won.' Thus it was presented as if uttered by Wellington whilst standing on those hallowed acres and it is this more than anything that destroys credibility in the assertion.

When Wellington was a pupil at the school not only were there no playing fields but there were no organised games at all. Secondly, he only revisited the place once, under protest, on an official engagement in 1841, and never left the shelter of the buildings during his abrupt stay. The whole thing originated in Montalembert's mind, he thinking that this was the sort of thing an Englishman would say about his *alma mater*.

Another attributed Wellingtonism is 'Up, Guards, and at 'em!', but fortunately for accuracy Wellington was still alive when this yarn was doing the rounds and, in a letter to John William Croker, he pooh-poohed the idea that he ever said any such thing when ordering the Guards against the French Imperial Guard. And, whilst not wishing to appear picky, when called upon to surrender this French unit did not send back a valiant galloper with the blood-stirring response of 'The Guard dies but never sur-renders'. Their reply was the somewhat more succinct – '*Merde*!'. As things turned out, the Guard did indeed surrender.

■　■　■

Attached to the English Civil War are some basic mis-conceptions regarding the Cavaliers and Roundheads.

Despite the image engendered by the film industry, very few of Cromwell's mob had short, cropped hair. Cromwell himself had shoulder-length hair as did his sons and most of his close associates and ministers. A limited number did go skinhead but these tended to be junior and overzealous types who only did so to draw stark contrast between themselves and the more flamboyant Royalists. It is probably also a fairly safe bet that there was an intention to convey austerity of character to boot.

Either way, the craze soon fizzled out and Lucy Hutchinson, a contemporary observer of events and detractor of Cromwell's wife, remarked that but a few years after the war the term Roundhead would have caused no little puzzlement. You see, the epithet had nothing to do with shaven heads but with the near spherical helmets favoured by the troops. It was, if you like, a bit like the British troops calling the Germans 'jerries' because their helmets resembled chamber pots.

During the conflict the city of Coventry was a Parliamentary stronghold and was used to hold secure important Royalist prisoners. All this went to ensure a significant military presence in the city which was strongly resented by the civilian population who were suitably taxed to maintain the situation. Any girl associating with troops had her head shaved and there was a well-entrenched and to a certain extent justified policy of non-fraternisation with the troops. This made Coventry an unpopular posting for the troops who equated being 'sent to Coventry' with being ostracised.

It is not possible to talk of Coventry without evoking the memory of Lady Godiva who, whilst a factual person, never cantered starkers through the streets. In the days of Godiva 'naked', as applied to a woman of her station, could also mean stripped of finery as befitting her station. If the ride ever did take place then she likely appeared in public presented as a woman of low station in common garb in order to humiliate her husband into lowering the taxes.

■ ■ ■

Long a nation given to strange pastimes, perhaps it is only the English who would engage in the peculiar ritual of Morris dancing, which is in fact a pale reflection of an ancient war dance of the Moors, whence the name.

It is thought that the ritual was brought back to England by the army of John O'Gaunt after his campaigns in Spain, where his men had seen such performances by the Moorish conscripts in the Spanish Army. Although present participants rap together little sticks the original dance involved swords and those who dropped the rhythm lost more than a few points for interpretation.

For the misconception that the Moors are a black race we have to thank countless generations of Shakespearian actors, all of whom have portrayed Othello by hamming it up like Al Jolson wrapped in a bed sheet. A fine-featured people with oval faces and hooked noses, the Moors are actually classified as a white race and the intrepid Scottish explorer, Mungo Park, makes mention in his writings of his life being saved several times in Africa through his having been mistaken for a Moor by potentially hostile natives.

As to the Shakespearian Othello, here we have a double misconception. Not only are Moors not black but the character upon which Shakespeare based his play was not even a Moor. Maurizio Othello was a white Venetian mercenary who had spent quite a bit of time in Hungary, where it is the custom to place the Christian name second. Thus there were several references to the man as Othello Mor, this latter being the Hungarian equivalent of Maurizio or Maurice. Thus it appears that Shakespeare made his mistake.

■ ■ ■

During the American Civil War one of the greatest scandals was the conditions within Andersonville prisoner-of-war camp, wherein were held upwards of 30,000 union soldiers. Only about 12,000 of these walked out alive. After the war the commanding officer, Captain Henry Wirz, stood trial for his war crimes and was duly hanged. Part of the trial concentrated on a line Wirz had drawn about the camp, running parallel with but several feet inside the main perimeter fence. Any inmate spotted in the no man's land betwixt the two was automatically assumed to be attempting to escape and shot out of hand. The name given to this line by the press was The Dead Line which has now come to represent a metaphorical limit by which time a task must be completed.

Back in the bankrupt South, several disillusioned Confederate officers and privates banded together to form an organisation intent on restraining the blacks from benefiting from any aspect of their new found 'liberty'. So was born the Ku Klux Klan at Pulaski, Tennessee, in May 1866. The club opted for such name basing it on the Greek *kyklos*, a circle, and adopted the emblem of the burning cross from the heyday of the clans in the Scottish Highlands. Known to the highlanders as The Fiery Cross, this was the symbol hoisted to rally the clans to battle and to ignore its call meant dishonour and death.

The bull-whip was a favourite tool employed by the Klan to drive back the newly enfranchised blacks from the polling stations, and at the time a heavy-calibre pistol or such a whip was widely known as a bull doser, since they were perceived as being capable of issuing sufficient violence to quell a bull. This earned the Klansmen the nickname of Bulldosers and when the first earth-moving machines appeared they acquired the nickname in the altered form of bulldozer through the association of driving back all before them. Incidentally a bull-whip did not acquire its name for its use on such animals but for their handles traditionally being made from a certain part of the bull's anatomy – bull-pizzle was an alternative name and defined by the OED as 'the penis of an animal, often that of a bull, formerly used as a flogging instrument.'

■ ■ ■

We have most of us experienced the clutches of a maiden aunt liberally doused in 4711 cologne and we have the Napoleonic forces to thank for both the perfume and the trade name.

In 1792 the Cologne family of Ferdinand Mulhens were happily churning out an innocuous little scent from a recipe they claim was given them by a grateful Carthusian monk to whom they had given refuge. If the Mulhens and others are to be believed then all of Europe was once teeming with monks and displaced princes who had no other means of securing sanctuary than by parting with some recipe for a perfume or liquor which they just happened to have on them at the time. You can just imagine it, can't you; a noble having to flee the mob screaming 'The hell with the jewels and gold, just grab the recipe for Drambuie, and let's go.'

No matter. The Mulhens were marketing under the name *Aqua Mirabilis* when the city fell to the Napoleonic force of occupation in 1794. The French billeting officers and military police found the city's maze of tiny streets and numbering system an absolute nightmare so they simply re-numbered every dwelling in the city in consecutive order and, you've guessed it, the Mulhens old address of 13 Glockengasse (Bell Lane) became house number 4,711.

The perfume found favour with the French officers' wives and soon quantities were being shipped back to Paris where the Cologne's name became synonymous with light perfumed waters. The Mulhens registered their imposed address as a trade mark but if you take a close look at the label you can still see a tiny bell above the numbers, this being a sentimental reminder of the old address.

Etymologically speaking, 'perfume' has a pretty unpleasant origin. The term first denoted scented wood burnt along with bits and pieces of a sacrificial victim in order to mask the smell of burning flesh which the 'congregation' found distasteful. The word is built on the Latin *per fuma*, through smoke.

■ ■ ■

At one time the border town of Berwick-upon-Tweed changed hands between the English and the Scottish with such monotonous regularity that our enemies –

and they were many – took to mentioning it specifically as being included or excluded in the forthcoming rumble. This was fine except that after we made peace with the Russians following the Crimean War, no one remembered to include Berwick in the treaty, resulting in the town remaining at war with Russia until 1966 when Moscow sent a delegation to Berwick to bury the hatchet.

One of the most flamboyant characters remembered from the Crimean War is Florence Nightingale, but in reality the Lady of the Lamp enjoyed a nursing career spanning a mere 600-odd days after which she took to her bed for fifty-four years, a hopeless hypochondriac and drug addict much given to the old laudanum bottle. Enshrined in her bed she was a totally self-centred, bullying tragedy queen who would immediately lapse into hyper-ventilation and palpitations the moment anyone dared disobey her slightest whim. Throughout these years her most devoted attendant was her aunt Mai, who had the temerity to return to her own home town for her daughter's wedding which resulted in Nightingale refusing to speak to her for the next twenty years because of Mai's sin of 'abandoning her post'.

■ ■ ■

While serving in India in 1875, Colonel Sir Neville Chamberlain (no relation to Neville 'I have in my hand a piece of paper' Chamberlain) was stationed at Jubbulpore and, bored by all the existing table games, devised snooker by drawing on pool, pyramids and billiards. The name arose from a casual remark made by the game's creator when he and some fellow officers were playing the game.

Probably based on 'snooks', the nose-thumbing derisive gesture, the term 'snooker' had for some time been common in Army slang to describe a new cadet at the Royal Military Academy, Woolwich, many of whose alumni were at Jubbulpore. On the night in question Chamberlain mocked an officer who failed to pot a ball that was hanging over a pocket by saying: 'Why, you're a regular snooker!' Several officers present were ignorant of the term's application and needed it explaining to them. Chamberlain is recorded as saying in a conversation many years later with Compton Mackenzie that, having explained his comment, he felt obliged to soothe the relevant officer's feathers by adding that, since the game itself was new, they were all 'snookers'.

The activities of turn-of-the-century troops in India gave rise to those of irrational behaviour being described as doolally, or suffering from doolally tap. Located outside Bombay, Deolali was both a military sanatorium and a staging camp for troops who had finished their tour of duty and were awaiting transport home. These men had no formal duties and the time that hung heavy on their hands was invariably spent drinking, gambling and just generally getting into trouble. In Hindustani *tap* meant a fever which also led to the insane being referred to as 'tapped'.

■ ■ ■

To eighteenth/nineteenth-century German or Prussian troops, the great coat was affectionately named Mathilde because 'she' kept them warm at night. When not required as a garment the coat was rolled and slung across the back like a bed roll which swayed side to side as the troops marched. This emerged in later Australian culture as 'waltzing matilda' in reference to the swagman's bed roll swinging jauntily from side to side as he went walkabout.

With a certain perversity troops have long given female names to the tools of their trade which, believe it or not, produced the 'mangle' as once favoured on wash day. The ultimate source is the old Prussian *manga*, a prostitute, but especially one who was attractive and exciting. This gave rise to the army referring to their early catapults as manganons, the throwing arms of which were drawn down with a crank-handle similar to that on the wash-day machine. When the first cannon made its impact the Germans likewise named it Gunhilda, this rapidly shortening to 'gun'.

Etymologically speaking, the carbine has the strangest history of all in that it takes its name from the dung beetle. In ancient Rome the troops detailed to remove the bodies of plague victims from the city were nicknamed the Scarabini since, like the scarab beetle, they rolled away all the rubbish. In medieval Italy certain regiments of light-mounted skirmishers were found to be still bearing the name in the altered form of Carabinieri. As fire arms spread in use the cavalry found they had no use for long-barrelled weapons and so specialised with short rifles – *violà* 'carbine'.

Multi-barrelled pistols were not uncommon, holding anything up to seven or eight shots and requiring the barrel complex to be rotated to bring each charge under the flintlock. For additional defence there was also a hefty brass guard encasing the firer's knuckles so that any surviving adversary could be battered to the ground. The seal on the firing chambers was not all that it should be, causing the owner's hand to become covered with powder burns. This earned the pistols the name of pepperpots or knuckledusters, this latter term still being heard today to describe the brass knuckles beloved of all good Millwall supporters.

■ ■ ■

More Miscellanea

Whilst it is true that Peter fulfilled the prophesy and denied Christ three times before cock-crow, this has nothing to do with 'to peter out' as is sometimes maintained. On the other hand, one thing this denial did produce was a ninth-century Papal decree requiring all churches to sport a cockerel weather vane as a reminder to all to keep the faith. It is odd indeed that the Vatican likes to claim its authority and tradition from the one who bottled out, but there we are.

In the nineteenth-century mining industry gunpowder was the main blasting medium and, since saltpetre was the main ingredient, the explosive was affectionately known as Peter. When a mine had been exploited to the full and all the goodies had been extracted, it was said to have been petered out. This usually meant that the firemen had finally blasted right 'down to bed-rock', this also remaining with us to describe being 'stony' broke.

Although now largely outmoded, 'peterman' is still understood to mean a man who blows safes – well, it is in certain sectors of society.

■　■　■

Forget what you have seen in cartoons, boa constrictors do not crush their victims to a pulp; they are far more parsimonious with their energy. Every time the prey exhales the snake simply takes up the slack in its coils and then locks off again. Eventually there is no expansion room left for the captive to inhale and death is from suffocation, not ruptured intestines and internal haemorrhage.

The only thing about the constrictors that has not been grossly exaggerated is their unbelievable strength. If a fully grown python took it into its head to kill an ox, then this it could accomplish without turning a hair, or a scale, rather. But the creatures only kill what they can swallow whole – and whole oxen hardly come into that category. Nor, for that matter, does man, but more of that later.

The upper size limit for both anacondas and pythons is about thirty feet, but just under twenty is the norm. The few anacondas that have reached the upper limit are condemned to remain in the water for life for they are no longer capable of efficient locomotion on land. Although ridiculous claims of sightings of 200 feet monsters persist they can safely be ignored. As the *Guinness Book of Animal Facts and Feats* puts it, 'Unfortunately many people forget that all animals must live within the laws of physics and chemistry.' The same chapter points out that the internal organs remain of uniform size and therefore progressively smaller and smaller in relation to increased body size. There will come a point beyond which these organs can no longer cope, and, in the cast of the constrictors, this point will come a long way before a body size of forty feet, let alone 200 feet.

As for the image of gargantuan serpents gulping down a couple of bwanas for hors-d'oeuvres, this can only happen in Tarzan films. There have been a couple of authenticated cases in which small children have met with such a hideous end, but although these creatures most certainly could kill a grown man, they most certainly could not eat him. If the snake started swallowing from the head then the shoulders would stick in the gullet. If it attempted to consume from the feet first the snake would require the intelligence to manoeuvre both legs together to avoid encountering a major problem in the middle of dinner. The python does not possess such intelligence, and even if it did, it could still get blocked at the shoulders.

▪ ■ ▪

It is a matter of individual choice whether or not to believe that there are those amongst us who can gaze out across the millenia and foretell with terrifying accuracy that which is going to befall the planet and its petty occupants. Be that as it may, there never was a Mother Shipton and most of her better known prophesies were made up for her years after her 'death'.

Supposedly born in 1488, Mother Shipton is first mentioned in 1641 in a tract that hails her as having predicted many things, including the rise to power of Cardinal Wolsey. Whoever it was that concocted this rubbish was not overly adventurous in that he only credited her with the foretelling of events between her supposed death and 1641. In other words the forger stuck safely to things that had already happened.

So, this con-man did not attempt any vicarious crystal-gazing on Ma Shipton's behalf, but others did.

All the guff about her having foretold of the advent of the telegraph, the steam engine, submarines and metal ships is rooted in prophesies written for her by a London-based publisher and bookseller called Charles Hindley. Unfortunately for the gullible, one of Hindley's little ravings had stated, quite clearly, that the world was going to end on 31 December 1881. Despite his fairly well published confession eight years before, that night in 1881 saw the gullible quitting their homes in droves to spend their last hours in solemn prayer in the fields, only to feel cheated and let down by the continuance of their lives.

People are forever stating that Nostradamus foretold of this or that with dazzling clarity and accuracy. But anyone who takes the trouble to go back to the original texts will find nothing of the kind. Michel de Notre Dame, as he was properly named, took great care to be as obscure as possible so that he could mean all things to all men. The big advantage here is that no one can pillory you for getting it cataclysmically wrong if no one is sure exactly what you did say in the first place.

It must be remembered that he was writing in the 1500s when the finger of heresy and witchcraft was pointed all too eagerly by a Church much given to the capricious incineration of anyone who irked or disagreed. The 'prophet' wrote in a jumble of Latin and Old French and resorted to anagrams and old runic symbols. In short, it was a load of old etheria into which you could read anything you wanted. But why knock him for that, Bob Dylan made a fortune in the sixties and seventies out of the same king's clothes lyrics.

■ ■ ■

Countless reference books – including the new edition of the *Oxford English Dictionary* – unreservedly credit W. A. Spooner, one-time Warden of Oxford's New College, with the birth of the so-called spoonerism. Among the admittedly funny jumbles that have been shoved into the dear old gentleman's mouth are reference to the Lord as a shoving leopard and the tale that he once rose to his feet to call on his fellow diners to raise a glass and drink a toast to 'The queer old Dean'. Given Oxbridge's reputation, personally, I do not see this as a spoonerism at all, but that's another matter.

On 22 July 1924, then at the ripe old age of eighty, Spooner made the following statement whilst being interviewed by the London *Evening Standard*: 'I suppose you really want to know the latest spoonerism. Well, it might interest you to know that I do not think that I have ever intentionally made a so-called spoonerism in my life, and in fact, I don't remember ever having made one. I know that it is a very sad thing to destroy the illusions of England in this way, but this is a thing that is true.' Tho sere!

■ ■ ■

As were so many of the nursery rhymes, the one relating the deeds of Little Jack Horner is based in fact and is essentially political satire.

The original Horner was steward to Richard Whiting, the Abbot of Glastonbury, turning out to be the last of his kind. After the Vatican tired of Henry VIII's voracious appetite for wives and his revolutionary approach to divorce, Rome broke ties with the monarch, causing Henry to be the first man to get the Abbey habit, but in a big way. Although it was referred to by the nicety of Dissolution of the Monasteries, what it boiled down to at the end of the day was Henry's minions touring the country killing all the monks and stealing their property. But, fair's fair, that's how the monks got most of it in the first place.

Against this backdrop Whiting sent Horner to the Court with the title deeds for twelve manors he owned in Somerset. The idea was to offer these *sans* aggro in the hope that Henry would be satisfied with that and leave the Glastonbury property alone. That Horner transported these documents to court, quite literally inside a pie dish covered with crust is not at all impossible; this was then a traditional manner of presenting something to someone as a sweetener.

Anyway, it was a nice idea but all was to no avail. As soon as he arrived at court the first thing that Horner did was to agree to enter into a conspiracy to have his boss stitched up on capital charges of treason. Whiting was immediately arrested and dragged off to London for a quickie show-trial before taking the long walk. And, guess who was sitting on the jury – none other than our old friend Horner.

Immediately after Whiting had gone to the big

cathedral in the sky, Horner – and three other honest jurors – took up residence in four of the twelve properties sent to placate the king. This will be the plum that Horner pulled out with his thumb and there is a local Somerset rhyme that puts it even more in focus. Two of the lines read as follows: 'Wyndham, Horner, Popham and Thynne, When the Abbots were dead they moved in.'

Horner's direct descendants still occupy Mells Manor in Somerset and, quite rightly, point out that their dodgy ancestor was forenamed Thomas and not Jack. But anyone in that era who was considered a knave was automatically referred to as Jack, as we still do with the knave of cards. The family also rather coyly maintain that Thomas bought the place on the up and up for the sum of £1,831 9s 1¾d, but we are talking about the days when you could fill up the donkey, take your girlfriend out for a venison and chip supper and still have change out of a groat. In other words, the guy paid nearly an Archer for the place, which in those days was one hell of a lot of money – and how would a mere steward get his hands on money like that honestly?

■ ■ ■

Traffic islands originated in Liverpool in 1862, thanks to a saddler, John Hastings; he had been campaigning for them for years. As usual, it took the death of a prominent citizen on the very spot that Hastings had been warning about for years before the idea was adopted. As long as it is only we peasants getting mown down, little or nothing gets done – but that's by the way.

London and all the other cities lagged behind and, curiously, the capital's first traffic island was built and installed privately in 1864 by one Colonel Pierpoint who had grown weary of doing a Pinball Wizard through the traffic to get to his club in St James, so he built his own mid-point refuge. Sadly for the safety-conscious Colonel his little idea backfired. One night he was crossing back with a fellow clubman when he succumbed to the folly of looking back over his shoulder at his brain-child whilst singing its praises to his companion. He walked straight under a speeding taxi and was killed.

■ ■ ■

The American Indian's contribution to the eating habits of the Western world is more significant than you might think!

In 1853 an Indian called George Crumm was the head chef (chief chef, if you like) at Moon's Hotel in Saratoga Springs, New York. His ultra-thin Saratoga chips, as he called them, were the talk of the town and they were of particular interest to one travelling businessman in particular who thought there might be a buck or two in flogging them cold in paper bags. His name was Frank – yes, you've guessed it – Smith.

The humble crisp was introduced into Britain some time around 1900 and had salt as an option in a blue twist of paper. This had to be done for the British market, not for matters of taste, but to meet legal requirements. Ready salted crisps were excluded by the old regulations dating back to the days of the gin mills when the house served free, heavily salted pork or mutton slices to keep the punters drinking. For a long time the use of salt on licensed premises was closely restricted until the amendments to the Licensing Act made in 1965.

▪ ▪ ▪

The original cadger was a country peddler who bought dairy produce from farms and retailed it at a small profit to earn a meagre living supplemented by begging. They took their name from the large basket, or cadge, from which they hawked their wares and, since cadgers were always whining for a hand-out, the term took on its current meaning.

Funnily enough, 'bread' and 'bribe' were once interchangeable terms since the latter meant nothing more sinister than a slice or lump of bread. In time, bribe shifted to refer specifically to bread given to beggars to stop them whining. The term moved to cover the sum of money given to the beggar to get him to go away and buy bread. 'Bribe' thus started down its slippery slope.

▪ ▪ ▪

Games resembling tennis were once played with the flat of the hand, so 'racquet' is derived from the Arabic *rahet* meaning the palm of the hand.

In medieval England a knockabout tennis was

played in courtyards where the columns and pillars formed natural obstacles, hence 'knocked from pillar to post'. The old French *bander* meant to knock a ball to and fro, hence 'to bandy words'. As for the name 'tennis', this most likely derives from the French *tenez*!, a court call meaning 'hold yourself ready to receive service'. 'Deuce' is a corruption of the French *deux*, two, since two more points are required. 'Love' is derived from *l'oeuf*, the egg, a shape suggesting zero.

'Jeopardy' comes from *jeu parti*, divided or equal game on points, where both parties are in danger of losing.

■ ■ ■

Although associated with hot climates, malaria was once common here. The name means 'bad air' since people knew it was somehow linked to foul swamps. To the British colonial service – ripping off, I mean, devoting their lives to improving the lot of, the poor in India – malaria was a serious problem until the advent of quinine powder.

Unfortunately, this tasted so horrible that it had to be added to a special fizzy drink to make it palatable. The grateful *sahibs* found the addition of gin to be the right way to make the medicine go down. Thus was born the noble gin and tonic, the drink upon which the sun never set while Britannia waived all the rules. Quinine is still added to tonic waters, albeit in much smaller quantities.

■ ■ ■

In medieval Italy most money-lenders operated from a bench and table in the market place. The Italian for a bench is *banco*, hence the modern 'bank'. If a money lender became insolvent, public officials performed a little ceremony that was as subtle as an air-raid. To indicate his financial state to one and all, they smashed up his bench with hammers. Notices were then posted declaring that the trader had been declared *bancorotto*, or 'broken bench'; we now say bankrupt.

Another expression synonymous with bankrupt is 'to go to the dogs'. It has no association with scraps being thrown to the dogs or, for that matter, any canine connection whatsoever. Our saying is just a corruption of the Old Dutch business maxim *toe goe, toe de dogs*, meaning 'money gone, credit gone'.

■　■　■

The number of dud shells fired by the British at the Somme resulted in the restricted hours in our pubs. Before the First World War, pubs opened at 6am and shut when they pleased. Consequently, many of the munitions workers were turning up blotto.

Each production crew had a shift quota to fulfil, and shells were being bodged either through drunkenness or the rush to get back to the pub. Lloyd George decided that enough was enough and brought in the first legislation to curtail opening hours. Also, under the Prohibition of Treat Act, it was illegal to buy, or offer to buy, a drink for a soldier or a war-effort worker, or to encourage heavy drinking by buying rounds. Unfortunately for misers, that Act was repealed after the war.

■ ■ ■

The expression 'gone for a Burton' is often assumed to relate in some way to Burtons the tailors. However, the accepted theory ties the expression to Burton Ales, which ran a particular advertising campaign just before the Second World War. Each poster showed an identifiable group of people – an orchestra or whatever – with one central figure obviously missing and his absence causing consternation. The never changing caption was 'He's gone for a Burton.'

The Royal Air Force adopted the caption, which first related only to pilots shot down over water – the sea being known as 'the drink'. It later became a euphemism in the Mess for any missing pilot.

■ ■ ■

Countless reference books talk about bears hibernating, so perhaps someone ought to tell the bears! They do go into a kind of torpor in the cold season, but do not experience the drop in heart-beat and metabolic rate which indicates the true hibernator. Bears laid up for the winter in caves can be easily woken and become alarmingly active, as many have found out to their terminal surprise.

The only member of the bear family that has anything in common with hibernators is the brown bear. It refrains from eating and drinking throughout its long rest but even so experiences protracted periods of wakefulness. An old folk myth tells that bear cubs are born completely without form and have to be 'moulded' by their mother, hence the expression 'licked into shape'.

▪ ▪ ▪

Rivers were of great importance in the ancient world since they formed natural boundaries. The names of several rivers live on in English. The Meander, now called the Drillo in modern Italy, was famed for its erratic wandering course. In mythology, the waters of the River Lethe in the underworld held the power to make all those who drank forget their worldly ties and lounge around Hades in a stupor, hence 'lethargic'.

The taking of an irrevocable step is called 'crossing the Rubicon' because that was the river separating Julius Ceasar's province of Cisalpine Gaul from Italy. As he marched towards Rome in 49BC there was much hurried negotiation but when he actually crossed the river at the head of his army Rome automatically interpreted this as an open declaration of war.

▪ ▪ ▪

The modern farce takes its name from the French *farcir*, to stuff or fill out, and is therefore a variant of 'force'. The term first described short, bawdy sketches put on to amuse the audience throughout the rather protracted intermissions in seventeenth-century plays. Either because these were 'stuffed' in between the main acts or because they padded out the performance, they were christened farces and gradually evolved into a form of their own.

As for pantomime, as the name suggests it was originally pure mime, but originally the word described not dumb theatre but that which mimicked or parodied ordinary life. From the Italian *commedia dell'arte* came the outrageous Giovanni, who was always acting the goat. The pet form of Giovanni is Zanni, from which the English derived 'zany'.

■ ■ ■

The word 'hybrid' is based on the Greek *hubris*, meaning violation, and first described a domestic sow who had been caught napping by a passing wild boar.

Hubris also means excessive pride and it was used in that sense in late nineteenth-century university slang. In Rome, a hybrid was a slave born of an enslaved woman and her master and such slaves tended to grow up slightly more 'Roman' than their mothers. Even so, their command of Latin was never perfect so, from *vernaculus*, born in one's master's house, there developed 'vernacular' which now describes informal and colloquial speech.

The much bandied about 'slang' remains a mystery. Conjecture has ranged from the Norwegian *slenjakeften*, to sling the jaw or verbally abuse another, to 'sling' as in tossed about. But no one knows the origin.

■ ■ ■

Cracking codes can be a mixed blessing. When British intelligence finally broke the German's Enigma code in 1940, the first transmission they intercepted warned of the impending heavy bombing of Coventry. Someone then had to decide whether or not to throw up defences and fighter cover and thus alert Germany to the fact that Enigma had been broken. Coventry got a pasting.

Fortunately for the Americans, their need of codes to use in the field was largely alleviated by using Red Indian wireless operators. These chatted away quite happily to each other in Kikkapoo, leaving the German listeners so much in the dark that the Indians used to wish them goodnight in English at the end of each transmission. Although most Indian languages include *hao*, which did mean hello, it was never used as a greeting, only as an exclamation of surprise.

■ ■ ■

There are as many myths attached to the hedgehog as there are spines to his back. They do not, for example, collect fallen fruit by rolling over, impaling it upon their armour before scurrying off to their dens. Why should they? The animal hardly ever eats fruit and since it hibernates it stores no food of any kind during winter. Next we have the endearing image of armies of hedgehogs trotting into the pastures at dawn to suck milk from the udders of sleeping cows. Hedgehogs have some pretty sharp teeth and if they latched on to an udder its owner would get up pretty smartly. No cow is going to lie quietly while some member of another species with needle-like gnashers munches away at its udders. What hedgehogs have been seen to do is to lap up milk that has leaked from the over-full udders of sleeping cows which is a different thing altogether.

It is perhaps inevitable that the sexual performance of a creature of such anatomical design should become the subject of jokes, speculation and misinformation. If hedgehogs encountered all the problems in mating that humans imagine, the poor little creature would have been extinct years ago. The female simply flattens her spines and they proceed as normal – normal for hedgehogs, that is. Nor is pain caused or damage done to the mother by the spines of the young during birth, for the very simple reason that the off-spring don't have any. At birth, the hedgehog's skin boasts only little pimples that are the spine sites but nothing starts growing until a couple of hours after delivery. Those that first appear are soft, white spines; the hard adult ones follow later.

Lastly, hedgehogs do not 'need' the fleas that infest them. This is the other edge of the sword that is their armour; it is impossible for the animal to rid itself of its unwelcome visitors. While it is true that the hedgehog seems to be able to live quite happily with its parasites, the creature would doubtless live a great deal happier life without them. Sometimes well-intentioned people have attempted to purge hedgehogs of infestation only to find their pets as dead as a dodo the next day. Such incidents went a long way to promote the idea that the hedgehog needed its fleas to survive. What had usually happened was the person concerned failed to realise that the decontaminating agent involved was as lethal to the host as to the parasites.

■ ■ ■

The peculiar statement in the Bible that discusses the relevant problems encountered by camels, needles and rich men wanting to check into the big counting house in the sky is a classic piece of mistranslation. It occurred when people first translated the book from Greek into English. The Greek for a rope is *kamilos* and the Greek for a camel is *kamelos*. The proper translation of the statement is that it is easier to thread a needle with a rope than for a rich man to enter the kingdom of heaven which makes a lot more sense, doesn't it?

Quite why God should be prejudiced against people with money has never been explained – churches certainly take enough of it on his behalf. On the other hand there is an old saying that states that if you want to know what God thought of money, just look at the people he gave it to.

Perhaps it is not surprising that such an extraordinary creature as the camel should find itself the subject of so many fallacies. Surely it is no longer necessary to state that the camel does not store water in its hump. Although, to be fair, there is by coincidence some indirect truth in the myth – for, when the fat that is stored in the hump is called upon as a food reserve, some water is produced in its digestion. The camel does store water, but does so in its stomach. This is lined with pouches, which fill up when the animal takes its formidable drinks (as much as twenty-five gallons at one time). The load in each pouch is retained by means of a sphincter muscle. The water is conserved because the camel's body temperature can go all the way up to the low hundreds before the animal even begins to sweat. Also, it urinates in very small quantities and very infrequently.

There is however, no chance for the camel to escape from the realms of myth for its parsimonious use of water has given birth to other fallacies about its abilities to survive without drinking. Suggestions of several weeks are absolutely ridiculous. A fully laden camel in the desert can go for three, possibly four, days without fresh water, but no more. Any assertions to the contrary are at best confused with the animal's capability under 'winter' conditions when, unladen, it can survive for about twenty days without drinking.

The camel is far from being the leader in the 'no water' stakes. The giraffe can go for months without drinking since it derives much of its moisture from its diet. The same applies to certain species of antelope. Nor have camel-hair brushes ever been made out of the rather coarse hair of the camel. They come from the tails of the Russian squirrel. How the camel became involved is a complete mystery.

■ ■ ■

In its military sense, 'tattoo' first came into vogue in the mid-seventeenth century in the Netherlands, where English troops were on active service during the interminable squabble with the Dutch. Due to the understandable hostility that Dutch civilians felt towards English troops occupying various areas of Dutch soil, it was considered wise to round up all the troops at 9pm. Basically this meant dragging them out of the pubs and marching them back to camp. A sort of 'last orders' drum squad used to march through the streets, playing a distinctive beat that called for all beer sales to English troops to cease. *Taptoe* – Dutch for 'the (beer) tap is shut' – became corrupted to 'tattoo' by the troops. Traditionally, military extravaganzas are opened by a drum corps and wound up by the playing of the tattoo beat. The Americans, incidentally, were satisfied with the first part of the original Dutch. This gave them 'Taps' which is now used at US military funerals.

As for the other tattoos, of the type favoured by the Navy, these are of Tahitian origin. They were introduced to the West by Captain Cook's South Seas voyage crew upon their return to England in 1796. The word is derived from the Polynesian *tatu*, which means a mark or design. The first of Cook's crew to place himself in the hands of the Tahitian graffiti merchants was appropriately named Robert Stainsby. Once the trend was established, sailors covered themselves in the abominations. One favourite design was a Crucifix in between the shoulders. This was tattooed there in the hope that the boatswain, when administering ship's punishment, would be reluctant to lay the cat too heavily across the face of Christ. There is no evidence that boatswains ever demonstrated any such restraint in swinging the cat – which takes us to the subject of cramped living quarters on board ship.

Punishment always took place on deck, because below there was quite literally 'not enough room to swing a cat'. The expression thus originally referred to the nine-tailed variety, not the nine-lived one. The reason that the flogging cat had nine tails was that this was considered a holy number, it being regarded as Trinity of Trinities. The idea was that a flogging with such a flail would be so much more purifying. There is no evidence that any sailor beaten half to death with it considered the experience to be in any way divine.

■ ■ ■

The next time that someone tells you that they can feel the ground shifting under their feet, believe them. It is. Our isle is actually rocking along a line that runs from about the middle of Devon up to the top right-hand corner of Yorkshire. Land to the right of the line is sinking, while that to the left is actually rising out of the sea.

Back in the year Something Hundred and Frozen Stiff, England was covered with millions upon millions of tons of ice which pressed the land-mass down. After the thaw England started to spring back into position in slow motion, like some sort of ginormous sponge. London, for example, is over fifteen feet lower than it was when the Romans came over to give us baths and straight roads. As a result, the River Thames is subject to tides for a full twenty miles further up than it was during the occupation.

On the other side of the coin, Harlech Castle, which was built in Wales in 1286, was once accessible from the sea. Now the water lies over half a mile away over rolling grass headlands.

If you want to pick up some easy money this week, bet someone that John O'Groats and Land's End aren't the most northerly and southerly points of the mainland. The most extreme tips are Dunnet's Head and Lizard Point respectively. If you really want to take your friends to the cleaners, give them a chance to get even with a bet as to the names of the most eastern, western, northern and southern of the American states. Just to lull them into a false sense of security give them an atlas. Don't worry, you're not going to lose. Ten to one they will confidently pronounce Maine as the most eastern, Florida as the most southern and Alaska as the most northern and western. Brushing aside their outstretched and expectant hands, point out that Hawaii took statehood in 1950 and is the most southern and, stupid as it might sound, Alaska qualifies on the other three compass points. It must be remembered that America is awfully wide and Alaska doesn't even begin until the 140-degree meridian. Many of the Aleutian Islands, which are part of Alaska, extend well beyond the 180-degree meridian which divides the eastern and the western hemispheres, so there are parts of Alaska many hundreds of miles further east than the eastern seaboard of America.

■ ■ ■